A New Pléiade

A New Pléiade

selected poems

Seven American Poets

Fred Chappell

Kelly Cherry

R. H. W. Dillard

Brendan Galvin

George Garrett

David R. Slavitt

Henry Taylor

Louisiana State University Press

Baton Rouge 1998

Copyright © 1998 by Louisiana State University Press

Designer: Michele Myatt Quinn
Typeface: A Garamond
Typesetter: Wilsted & Taylor Publishing Services

Library of Congress Cataloging-in-Publication Data

Seven American Poets.
    A new pléiade : selected poems / [by] seven American poets ; Fred
Chappell . . . [et al.].
        p.   cm.
    Poems of Fred Chappell, Kelly Cherry, R.H.W. Dillard, Brendan
Galvin, George Garrett, David R. Slavitt, and Henry Taylor.
    ISBN 0-8071-2329-3 (cloth : alk. paper). — ISBN 0-8071-2330-7
(paper : alk. paper)
    1. American poetry.—20th century.   I. Chappell, Fred, 1936–
II. Title.
PS615.S387   1998
811'.5408—dc21   98-24404
                                                          CIP

The poets' photographs were taken by, respectively, Katharine Morse-Chappell, Meg Theno, the
Hollins College Office of Public Relations, Ellen Galvin, Jack Mitchell, Bernard Gotfryd, and Melissa
Laitsch.

The paper in this book meets the guidelines for permanence and durability of the Committee on
Production Guidelines for Book Longevity of the Council on Library Resources. ∞

Publisher's Note

This book celebrates the literary friendships that sustain and unite seven contemporary American poets. For decades, these seven have been meeting, corresponding, sharing, and supporting one another's work, so that while their poems always bear the stamp of their creative individuality, they also give witness to the generosity and productivity of their writerly intimacy. Louisiana State University Press has long enjoyed the privilege of bringing the work of each of these poets to readers' attention, and we now welcome the opportunity to present selections of all of them in an anthology that vividly attests to the poets' enduring association.

The impetus for the volume came from the poets themselves, and its form derives from an insouciant principle of selection that they decided on, viz., that the work of each poet would be chosen by the contributor whose name precedes his or hers alphabetically. Thus, Fred Chappell culled the following selection from the poems of Kelly Cherry, who in turn picked which poems would be included by R. H. W. Dillard, who chose the ones by Brendan Galvin, etc. In this way, the poets' variant ways of musing on one another's work inform the very contents of *A New Pléiade*.

For readers previously acquainted with the individual work of some or all of these seven, this volume will serve to reilluminate familiar poems by one rendered in conjunction with poems by the others. But a different sort of pleasure is proffered those readers who come newly to these poets' work: first impressions of one poet's voice and vision will develop together with those formed of the next read, and the next, so that in the midst of the poets' diversity will resonate the unity of their purpose.

for Les Phillabaum

Contents

KELLY CHERRY

R. H. W. DILLARD

BRENDAN GALVIN

George Garrett

David R. Slavitt

HENRY TAYLOR

FRED CHAPPELL

THE GARDEN

The garden is a book about the gardener.

His thoughts, set down in vivid greenery,
The white light and the gold light nourish.
Firm sentences of grapevine, boxwood paragraphs,
End-stops of peonies and chrysanthemums,
Cut drowsy shadows from the afternoon.

Out of their hiding places the humid twilight
Lures the stars. The perfumes of the grass
Draw like cool curtains across the mind
And what the mind is certain it is certain of.

So that the twilight fragrances are clearly audible,
The garden stroking the senses with slow roses.
Bats ramble overhead, tacking from star
To early star as if putting in at ports of call.
And then the Chinese lantern is lit as it was in childhood,
As central in that place as an island lighthouse.

The gardener is a book about his garden.
He walks among these leaves as easy as morning
Come to scatter its robins and tender noises.
As the plants inhale the morning and its cool light,
The book is open once again that was never shut.
What now we do not know we shall never know.

THE FIELDS

The hay, the men, are roaring on the hill.
July muzzy and itchy in the fields,
Sunlight opens its mouth on the tractor's drone,
Bumblebees like thumbs in the bolls of red clover.
Summer within the field, unsparing fountain

Of heat and raw savor.
                    The men redden and sweat,
Their torsos flash, the talk and the laughing jet up cool,
Single cool sound in the saffron air, air like a woolen cloak.
The land lies open, at the mercy of the trembling sun.
One cloud drives east; the cattle plunder the brackish pools,
Black flies fumble on their hides.
They chew, observe the hour with incurious eye.

Mouths agape, the men gulp fierce breath.
If now a breeze could lift the fields!
   . . . But their skins cloy with dust. Grin and gouge.
Neck muscles sore, exhaustion laps the bodies,
Their mouths are desperately open, fork-tines feint and plunge.
And then the woman brings the water, the clear jar
Echoing rings of light that flutter on her apron.

Now the wagon is heaped and going away.
Bronze-green hay like a shaggy skirt, the wagon
Halts then sways unsteady to the barn.
Bronze-green tongues of it leap to the sill.
They harry it in and the loft is bulging,
Surfeit beneath the tin roof of sheeted fire.
Mouse-gray pigeons march and croon,
Dipping beaks like shards of flower pots.

   . . . The hill bare now, blackbirds swoop in a sudden net,
Scatter like pepper specks. The men, those shouts of flesh,
Gone home to the wash basin, to the glowing table.
Slow dark: the mountains empurple and encroach.

Hay all in, tobacco now and corn
As the ground sleeps and cools, the barns huddle
At twilight, bats in the starry dusk like pendulums.
Goldenrod indolent, blue moonlets of chicory,
Queen Anne's lace precise as the first stars of frost.
Ponds grimace and show their teeth
As the winds tug the westward mountains.

The land, clenched shut.

Trees thrash, noble and naked wrestlers,
Clouds mass within and beneath the heavy winds.
The shining birds go away, but quail and bobwhite
Keep the drying pasture. Thistle spends its silver,
Frost drives through rind and pith.
                              The brittle season:
Crash crash of leaves in seemly groves;
Austerity of alders;
Blue grapes;
Last glimmer of crickets.

Then winter in the hearth.
The sizzling oak joint snaps like cap pistols
And the smoke rolls generous under the sky.
The grandaddy snorts and nods;
His chessboard idles while whiskey nudges his elbow.
All the rooms grow smaller, creak creak
The timbers mutter. House tightens and the roof howls.
Ice like cheesecloth on the still water;
Glass needles in the ground.
Rattles, clinks;
Clear rime.

The stupor of cold wide stars.

And in the narrowed fields the wind from dead north
Mauling the cattle together, furrowing hides
Red and white, sifts into the creases
First snow like moss. They moan at the gate,
Turning the whited eye. Spaces between boards
Ice-crusted, the barns let the blow in.
Sleet piddles the ridged roofs.
The sky is volumes of smeary grays, and flesh
Pinches and rasps, the skin chill and reluctant.

First deep snow then, and the sun blind on it,
Edges depart the customary to reveal their truth.

Nothing is stark. The light enlarges
Such a fearful blue the mind burns with pain,
Body feels evanescent as mist.
                              Night closes over,
Deep crucible merciless and songless.
The land creeps to star-marge,
Horizon cluttered with light,
                        indifferent emblem of eternity.

Nothing will move but the whisperless wheel of sky:

Axis that fixes and orders revolves on a hub of ice:

The houses burrow deeper and deeper.

The world: locked bone.

GRACE BEFORE MEAT

As this noon our meat we carve,
Bless us better than we deserve.

ANOTHER

Bless, O Lord, our daily bread.
Bless those in hunger and in need
Of strength. Bless all who stand in want.
Bless us who pray, bless us who can't.

How the Job Gets Done

A dust of rubble warriors whitens the plain
where the chariots plunged and shattered. The sleep
of bronze and the ceaseless memorial wind
caress those acres like a crop of wheat;

the rivers have carried away the mules flyblown
and bloated, the torn veils of the widows,
the hafts and dented greaves, the portable gods.
Insubordinate Thersites got seven solid years

latrine duty no one is marking now, except
the poet in his garden, laboring to line-end,
then turning back like a sweating plowman to fold
another loamy furrow over the crumbled palaces.

In the Garden

The guitar's rubato quivered
And died. The woman shivered
And lifted toward the night her head.
He set his wine glass on the tray.
There was something fragile they had feared to say.
Now it was said.

I Love You

Yet you were gone six days before
I took from the bedroom closet the dress,
The blue and white one that you wore
To that dinner party that was such a mess,
And fearfully hung it on the door,

And sat before it in a chair,
Remembering what and when and where,
And touched it with a ghost's caress.

TRANSMOGRIFICATION OF THE DIVA

May she lie sleeping still
While the disarranged powders dust the frayed
Pink crinkled ribbons adrift on mother-of-pearl.
The castrato cat at bedfoot dozes, his eyes
Plump-shut with drowse. She will not restlessly stir,
Half-open hands at peace.

Keep the squabbles of tenors
Far now from her whole rest; let the curtain rise
Over the pit, floodlight knifing above
The horns and varnished oboes; let Maestro
Carve the unfathomable score, while she
In-breathes the musk of time.

Let the audience yet crave
Her ghost-glimmer in the second act:
That sweet note the young soprano cannot form.
Let it then transpire: pure clean shaft
Of music open her breast to the trompe l'oeil skies
Where the gilt swans stream.

DIPPERFUL

"Help yourself to a drink, it's toted fresh."

My hand rose in the water to meet my hand
And in its shadow his sweet spring appeared.
Mica-grains swarmed out of the hill-womb,

A crawfish trailed a funnel of yellow sand.
I drank the hill. A scatter of sand-motes sparkled
When I launched the gourd's blind belly back in the bucket,
And on my tongue the green hill sprouted ferns.

Went back to jaw and ravel the afternoon
With the old man on his porch that shaded his hounds
Beneath, warm spotted lumps of doze and quiver.
I sat down easy to watch at ease the cornfield
Across the creek get tall.

                    "Been walking far?"

"Not half as far," I said, "as my feet would say."
He nodded and thumbed a twisted cigarette shut.
"Used to," he said, "I'd wear the daylight out,
I'd trudge till my cartridges was gone. I shot
To death I swear to God all of the pokeweed
In Johnson's pasture. That would keep me going.
A boy'll walk to the end of the world, not thinking."

"Sure. But when you had to walk to work—"

"—They couldn't inch me along with a twelve-pound sledge.
But if we didn't have the triflingness
To think back on, nobody would come this far."

"How far?"

            "Eighty years this coming December."   .
He spat and watched it roll up in the dust,
Leaned back, and thought the thoughts an old man thinks.
I felt myself slide off the edge of his mind.
Dreaming, he spoke. "What hinders my sleep most
Is my daddy's boots. Here they come a-sailing
At me when I shut my eyes, bobbing
Off the floor by his bedside, great things
That felt as hard as iron when I was a youngun.
The way he kept them candled, rubbing and rubbing

At night to keep the water out, the way
The upper hooks would shine like a black cat's eyes.
I'd ponder on them, how strong I'd have to be
When I got growed to march my boots along.
Can't I just hear him puffing whenever he'd bend
Over to lace them to the top? His hair
Flopped down on his face. He'd straighten up
And stare at nothing, the day that was coming ahead.

"I recall one time I reached my hand in there.
Jerked it out again, for that surprised me,
How hot his boots got, hot as fresh fire coals.
All day long the old man's walking in fire,
I thought, and thought I didn't want
To olden and walk in fire the way he did.
And I don't know I did, the way he did.
I never got married, you see, never had
To grub for other people. I worked enough
To keep myself a peaceful sufficiency.
The world ain't all that lonesome for more MacReadies.
Now I'm so busted down there ain't much left,
But not a burden to some old muley woman."

He spat again and a swoon of flies unsettled,
Then settled back. The early afternoon
Began to climb the fields. "I've talked too much,"
He said. "I wish I didn't talk so much."
When he said that, the silence had its say.

THE READER

for Helene Nicholls

Beside the floor lamp that has companioned her
For decades, in her Boston rocking chair,
Her body asks a painful question of the books.

Her fingers are so smooth and white
They reflect the pages; a light
The color of cool linen bathes her hands.
The books read into her long through the night.

There is a book that opens her like a fan: and so
She sees herself, her life, in delicate painted scenes
Displayed between the ivory ribs that may close up
The way she claps the book shut when she's through
The story that has no end but cannot longer go.
It doesn't matter what the story means;
Better if it has no meaning—or just enough
For her to say the sentence that she likes to say:
Why do these strange folks do the way they do?

And yet they comfort her, being all
That she could never be nor wish to be;
They bring the world—or some outlook of its soul—
Into her small apartment that is cozy
As the huddling place of an animal
No one is yet aware of, living in
A secret corner of a secret continent,
An animal that watches, wonders, while the moon
Rides eastward and the sun comes up again
Over a forest deep as an ocean and as green.

My Grandmother Washes Her Feet

I see her still, unsteadily riding the edge
Of the clawfoot tub, mumbling to her feet,
Musing bloodrust water about her ankles.
Cotton skirt pulled up, displaying bony,
Bruised, and patchy calves that would make you weep.

Rinds of her soles had darkened, breadcrust-colored—
Not yellow now—like the tough outer belly
Of a snake. In fourteen hours the most refreshment
She'd given herself was dabbling her feet in the water.

"You mightn't have liked John Giles. Everyone knew
He was a mean one, galloping whiskey and women
All night. Tried to testify dead drunk
In church one time. That was a ruckus. Later
Came back a War Hero, and all the young men
Took to doing the things he did. And failed.
Finally one of his women's men shot him."

"What for?"

       "Stealing milk through fences . . . That part
Of Family nobody wants to speak of.
They'd rather talk about strong men, brick houses,
Money. Maybe you ought to know, teach you
Something."

       "What *do* they talk about?"

            "Generals,
And the damn old Civil War, and marriages.
Things you brag about in the front of Bibles.
You'd think there was arms and legs of Family
On every battlefield from Chickamauga
To Atlanta."

       "That's not the way it is?"

"Don't matter how it is. No proper way
To talk, is all. It was nothing they ever did.
And plenty they never talk about . . . John Giles!"

Her cracked toes thumped the dingy tub wall, spreading
Shocklets. Amber toenails curled like shavings.
She twisted the worn knob to pour in coolness
I felt suffuse her body like a whiskey.

"Bubba Martin, he was another, and no
Kind of man. Jackleg preacher with the brains
Of a toad. Read the Bible sideways crazy
Till it drove him crazy, marking craziness
On doorsills, windows, sides of Luther's barn.
He killed hisself at last with a twelve-gauge shotgun.
No gratitude for Luther putting him up
For twenty years. Shot so's to fall down the well."

"I never heard."

           "They never mention him.
And not Aunt Annie, that everybody called
Paregoric Annie, that roamed the highways
Thumbing cars and begging change to keep
Even with her craving. She claimed to save up
To buy a glass eye. It finally shamed her sisters
Enough, they went together and got her one.
That didn't stop her. She toted it around
In a velvet-lined case, asking strangers
Please to drop it in the socket for her.
They had her put away. And that was that.
There's places Family ties just won't stretch to."

Born then in my mind a race of beings
Unknown and monstrous. I named them Shadow-Cousins,
A linked long dark line of them,
Peering from mirrors and chortling in closets, eager
To manifest themselves inside myself.
Like discovering a father's cancer.
I wanted to search my body for telltale spots.

"Sounds like a bunch of cow thieves."

"Those too, I reckon,
But they're forgotten or covered over so well
Not even I can make them out. Gets foggy
When folks decide they're growing respectable.
First thing you know, you'll have a Family Tree."

(I pictured a scraggy wind-stunted horse-apple.)

She raised her face. The moons of the naked bulb
Flared in her glasses, painting out her eyes.
In dirty water light bobbed like round soap.
A countenance matter-of-fact, age-engraved,
Mulling in peaceful wonder petty annals
Of embarrassment. Gray but edged with brown
Like an old photograph, her hair shone yellow.
A tiredness mantled her fine energy.
She shifted, sluicing water under instep.

"O what's the use," she said. "Water seeks
Its level. If your daddy thinks that teaching school
In a stiff white shirt makes him a likelier man,
What's there to blame? Leastways, he won't smother
Of mule-farts or have to starve for a pinch of rainfall.
Nothing new gets started without the old's
Plowed under, or halfway under. We sprouted from dirt,
Though, and it's with you, and dirt you'll never forget."

"No Mam."

"Don't you say me No Mam yet.
Wait till you get your own chance to deny it."

Once she giggled, a sound like stroking muslin.

FRED CHAPPELL

14

"You're bookish. I can see you easy a lawyer
Or a county clerk in a big white suit and tie,
Feeding the preacher and bribing the judge and sheriff.
Second-generation-respectable
Don't come to any better destiny.
But it's dirt you rose from, dirt you'll bury in.
Just about the time you'll think your blood
Is clean, here comes dirt in a natural shape
You never dreamed. It'll rise up saying, Fred,
Where's that mule you're supposed to march behind?
Where's your overalls and roll-your-owns?
Where's your Blue Tick hounds and Domineckers?
Not all the money there is can wash true-poor rich.
Fatback just won't change to artichokes."

"What's artichokes?"

                        "Pray Jesus you'll never know.
For if you do it'll be a sign you've grown
Away from what you are, can fly to flinders
Like a touch-me-not . . . I may have errored
When I said *true-poor.* It ain't never the same
As dirt-poor. When you got true dirt you got
Everything you need . . . And don't you say me
Yes Mam again. You just wait."

                             She leaned
And pulled the plug. The water circled gagging
To an eye and poured in the hole like a rat.
I thought that maybe their spirits had gathered there,
All my Shadow-Cousins clouding the water,
And now they ran to earth and would cloud the earth.
Effigies of soil, I could seek them out
By clasping soil, forcing warm rude fingers
Into ancestral jelly my father wouldn't plow.
I strained to follow them, and never did.
I never had the grit to stir those guts.
I never had the guts to stir that earth.

Third Base Coach

He commands as mysteriously
as the ghost of Hamlet's father.

Shuffles & tugs & yawns & spits.
Like a steeplejack he itches weirdly and continually.

Dances on his grave plot
as if the secrets in his head were Walkman music.

Writes runes with his toe.
The fouls go by him like tracer bullets.

Like an Aeschylean tragedy he's static,
Baffling, boring, but.
                              Urgent with import.

Strike Zone

for Joe Nicholls

Like the Presidency its size
depends upon the man.

The pitcher whittles at the casement,
trying not to bust the paneless window.

The batter peers into it like a peeping tom.
Is he excited by what he sees?

The limits get stricter
as they get less visible.

Throwing at yards and yards of Willie McCovey,
a foot or so

of Luis Aparicio,
the pitcher tries not to go bats.

Umpire knows a thing or two,
but gives no sign.

Ball 3.

SOME OF IT

Everybody got shot
They laid down in flags or came back in giblets
I sniveled after girls I couldn't get it up for
And fumbled the bottles over the chipped formica
And dreamed of debriefings and the wrong LZ coordinates

Roberto and Bill came by the ward to cheer me
But all I remember are teeth snapping like breech bolts
At last I told Dr. Will and his ugly nurse to shove it
And marched back to The Zulu Lounge to heal myself
After that for a year nothing comes clean to my head

I got some shit from a full disability hero
Who told me he'd killed a girl in Can Tho or Kansas
Or was it me that killed her, he had to ask
Detective Sgt. Rico told me to leave New Jersey
But slipped me a bottle of Rocket at the Trailways station

My bowels were busted, my molars glowed with pain
In the snow by the firebarrel I watched my footprints wander
I heard an old man bleeding under the trestle
And went to have a look and sure enough
I polished off the pint the corpse was deserting

I usually make believe I survived but now
When I dig my left hand through the mud of this blue ditch

I'm sure I feel something pumping that doesn't stop
It must be the mighty big whiskey heart of the world
The hot whiskey heart that makes the dying sociable

NARCISSUS AND ECHO

Shall the water not remember   *Ember*
my hand's slow gesture, tracing above   *of*
its mirror my half-imaginary   *airy*
portrait? My only belonging   *longing*
is my beauty, which I take   *ache*
away and then return as love   *of*
of teasing playfully the one being   *unbeing.*
whose gratitude I treasure   *Is your*
moves me. I live apart   *heart*
from myself, yet cannot   *not*
live apart. In the water's tone,   *stone?*
that shining silence, a flower   *Hour,*
whispers my name with such slight   *light,*
moment, it seems filament of air,   *fare*
the world become cloudswell.   *well.*

THE STORY

for Barbara Moran

Once upon a time the farmer's wife
told it to her children while she scrubbed potatoes.
There were wise ravens in it, and a witch
who flew into such a rage she turned to brass.

The story wandered about the countryside until
adopted by the palace waiting maids

who endowed it with three magic golden rings
and a handsome prince named Felix.

Now it had both strength and style and visited
the household of the jolly merchant
where it was seated by the fire and given
a fat gray goose and a comic chambermaid.

One day alas the story got drunk and fell
in with a bunch of dissolute poets.
They drenched it with moonlight and fever and fed it
words from which it never quite recovered.

Then it was old and haggard and disreputable,
carousing late at night with defrocked scholars
and the swaggering sailors in Rattlebone Alley.
That's where the novelists found it.

Upon an Amorous Old Couple

This coltish April weather
Has caused them to aspire
To rub dry sticks together
In hopes that they'll catch fire.

Wedding Anniversary

Gale winds tore this tree
And drought and frost came near
To killing it. But see:
In its thirtieth year
It blooms like a candleflame,
And puts its youth to shame.

The Epigrammatist

Mankind perishes. The world goes dark.
He racks his brain for a tart remark.

The Ubi Sunt Lament
of the Beldame Hen

Is there no one who can tell
The tales of heroes of olden days,
Their voices strong as the chapel bell?
When they strutted their stuff on straw runways,
Their plumage shed resplendent rays.
O where is noble Chanticleer
On whom the world adored to gaze?
Where are the cocks of yesteryear?

There was a rooster journeyed to hell,
Or so the ancient legend says,
Who conquered there and came back whole
To fill the world with strange amaze.
O Orpheus, in limp times like these
We need a champion who has no fear
To shame the devil to his face.
But where are the cocks of yesteryear?

Where are Hector and William Tell,
Veterans of a thousand frays?
Where is Ajax who never fell,
And had such polish, such winning grace,
He was the jewel of our race?
With eye so red and comb so rare,
His was the look that truly slays.
O where are the cocks of yesteryear?

This conundrum that I raise
Was broached of old by La Belle Heaulmière
In Master Villon's langue française:
Where are the cocks of yesteryear?

Susan, we've reached that mellow period
That offers a truly rare and curious pleasure:
We now look forward to looking back in leisure,
Fretting little the future present in God.
To fear the worst is not impiety,
Only a picklepuss ungraciousness
That adds no ornament to a happy day
And leaves a dreary day a turgid mess.

It's true that we begin to take precautions
As joints and sinews start to crack and creak
And intellectual powers grow kitten-weak
And social life avoids loud commotions.
But how can we regret a regimen
Enabling us to live as we had hoped
We someday would? We always had a plan,
One that evil years battered and scraped,

That now we resurrect as we approach
A time that makes it possible at last
To welcome Quiet as an honored guest
And listen to the poet Horace broach
Advice on how to spend the years to come.
He bids us not to worry, to drink some wine,
And in the lines that gave us *carpe diem*
Tells us to leave astrologers alone:

Let's not go prying, Susan, into forbidden
Knowledge; it's best our death dates remain hidden
From any calculating astrologer.
This winter, with its stone-destroying power,

May be our last; or maybe several more
God has allotted us.
                              —Be wise. Drink up.
Our brief lives shorten, wasted in long hope.
Now while we chat, the light hours fleet away.
Credit no tomorrow. *Seize the day.*

How better seized than to remember when
Our love was new and we were full of fear
And any thought might start a secret tear
Or any frown transform into a grin?
There's not much fun in being mostly broke
At an expensive university,
And loony Fred was the most improvident bloke
To have to face such square adversity.

But we got by, through your deft management,
And read the books and wrote the dumb exams
And watched some friends go down in angry flames
While others settled in with sweet content.
My ambitions were to write poetry
And make a modest living teaching school,
Happy to suffer the Eighteenth Century
And week on week of tuna casserole.

—That's why I waste no precious cerebration
In choosing for our salad memory herbage;
Too many years we spent in pinchpurse curbage.
It's time to pop the corks of celebration.
Let us accompany our choice greens
With fresh-baked loaves of chewy Italian bread
And open a variety of wines,
A California white, a Spanish red,

A Provençal rosé, a light Bordeaux,
Perhaps a muscat from the upper Loire,
A German Riesling to lend its nimble air,

And one dark bottle of earthy staunch Margaux.
And on the side we'll set a plate of cheese:
Red Leicester, Roquefort, and an aged Cantal
If we can find it, several creamy Bries,
A runny Camembert with lots of soul.

These will make our salad memorable
For our anniversary déjeuner
Beneath our oak trees where the hastening day
Makes even mortal thoughts quite beautiful.
A skimpy dressing of oil and lemon juice—
A spackle of leaf-shadowed noonday sun
Give the pepper mill three hearty screws
And our spring garden salad is quite done.

HUMILITY

In the necessary field among the round
Warm stones we bend to our gleaning.
The brown earth gives in to our hands, and straw
By straw burns red aslant the vesper light.

The village behind the graveyard tolls softly, begins
To glow with new-laid fires. The children
Quiet their shouting, and the martins slide
Above the cows at the warped pasture gate.

They set the tinware out on checkered oilcoth
And the thick-mouthed tumblers on the right-hand side.
The youngest boy whistles the collie to his dish
And lifts down the dented milk pail.

This is the country we return to when
For a moment we forget ourselves,
When we watch the sleeping kitten quiver
After long play, or rain comes down warm.

Here we might choose to live always, here where
Ugly rumors of ourselves do not reach,
Where in the whisper-light of the kerosene lamp
The deep Bible lies open like a turned-down bed.

FOREVER MOUNTAIN

J. T. Chappell, 1912–1978

Now a lofty smoke has cleansed my vision.

I see my father has gone to climb
Lightly the Pisgah slope, taking the time
He's got a world of, making spry headway
In the fresh green mornings, stretching out
Noontimes in the groves of beech and maple.
He has cut a walking stick of second-growth hickory,
And through the amber afternoon he measures
Its shadow and his own shadow on a sunny rock.
                    Not marking the hour, but observing
The quality of light come over him.
He is alone, except what voices out of time
Swarm to his head like bees to the bee-tree crown,
The voices of former life as indistinct as heat.

By the clear trout pool he builds his fire at twilight,
And in the night a granary of stars
Rises in the water and spreads from edge to edge.
He sleeps, to dream the tossing dream
Of the horses of pine trees, their shoulders
Twisting like silk ribbon in the breeze.

He rises glad and early and goes his way,
Taking by plateaus the mountain that possesses him.

My vision blurs blue with distance,
I see no more.
Forever Mountain has become a cloud
That light turns gold, that wind dislimns.

This is continually a prayer.

MY GRANDMOTHER WASHES HER VESSELS

In the whitewashed medical-smelling milkhouse
She wrestled clanging steel; grumbled and trembled,
Hoisting the twenty-gallon cans to the ledge
Of the spring-run (six by three, a concrete grave
Of slow water). Before she toppled them in—
Dented armored soldiers booming in pain—
She stopped to rest, brushing a streak of damp
Hair back, white as underbark. She sighed.

"I ain't strong enough no more to heft these things.
I could now and then wish for a man
Or two . . . Or maybe not. More trouble, likely,
Than what their rations will get them to do."

The August six-o'clock sunlight struck a wry
Oblong on the north wall. Yellow light entering
This bone-white milkhouse recharged itself white,
Seeped pristine into the dozen strainer cloths
Drying overhead.

                    "Don't you like men?"

Her hand hid the corner of her childlike grin
Where she'd dropped her upper plate and left a gap.
"Depends on the use you want them for," she said.
"Some things they're good at, some they oughtn't touch."

"Wasn't Grandaddy a good carpenter?"

She nodded absentminded. "He was fine.
Built churches, houses, barns in seven counties.
Built the old trout hatchery on Balsam . . .
Here. Give me a hand."

               We lifted down
Gently a can and held it till it drowned.
Gushed out of its headless neck a musky clabber
Whitening water like a bedsheet ghost.
I thought, Here spills the soldier's spirit out;
If I could drink a sip I'd know excitements
He has known; travails, battles, tourneys,
A short life fluttering with pennants.

                    She grabbed
A frazzly long-handled brush and scrubbed his innards
Out. Dun flakes of dried milk floated up,
Streamed drainward. In his trachea water sucked
Obscenely, graying like a storm-sky.

"You never told me how you met."

                      She straightened,
Rubbed the base of her spine with a dripping hand.
"Can't recollect. Some things, you know, just seem
To go clear from your mind. Probably
He spotted me at prayer meeting, or it could
Have been a barn raising. That was the way
We did things then. Not like now, with the men
All hours cavorting up and down in cars."

Again she smiled. I might have sworn she winked.

"But what do you remember?"

                    "Oh, lots of things.
About all an old woman is good for

Is remembering. . . . But getting married to Frank
Wasn't the beginning of my life.
I'd taught school up Greasy Branch since I
Was seventeen. And I took the first census
Ever in Madison County. You can't see
It now, but there was a flock of young men come
Knocking on my door. If I'd a mind
I could have danced six nights of the week."

We tugged the cleaned can out, upended it
To dry on the worn oak ledge, and pushed the other
Belching in. Slowly it filled and sank.

"Of course, it wasn't hard to pick Frank out,
The straightest-standing man I ever saw.
Had a waxed moustache and a chestnut mare.
Before I'd give my say I made him cut
That moustache off. I didn't relish kissing
A briar patch. He laughed when I said that,
Went home and shaved. . . . It wasn't the picking and saying
That caused me ponder, though. Getting married—
In church—in front of people—for good and all:
It makes you pause. Here I was twenty-eight,
Strong and healthy, not one day sick since I
Was born. What cause would I have to be waiting
On a man?"

                    Suddenly she sat on the spring-run edge
And stared bewildered at empty air, murmuring.

"I never said this to a soul, I don't
Know why . . . I told my papa, 'Please hitch me
The buggy Sunday noon. I can drive
Myself to my own wedding.' That's what I did,
I drove myself. A clear June day as cool
As April, and I came to where we used to ford
Laurel River a little above Coleman's mill,
And I stopped the horse and I thought and thought.
If I cross this river I won't turn back. I'll join

To that blue-eyed man as long as I've got breath.
There won't be nothing I can feel alone
About again. My heart came to my throat.
I suppose I must have wept. And then I heard
A yellowhammer in a willow tree
Just singing out, ringing like a dance-fiddle
Over the gurgly river-sound, just singing
To make the whole world hush to listen to him.
And then my tears stopped dropping down, and I touched
Nellie with the whip, and we crossed over."

HALLOWIND

> *Setting:* Halloween, 1961; Durham, N.C.
> *Personae:* Reynolds Price, Susan, Fred, the rain, the wind

Fred
Listen to it skirl the roof
And tear the ragged eaves as if
The world outside weren't room enough!

Reynolds
Voices.

Fred
What do they say?

Reynolds
                    "In, in."
The ghosts of stories not yet written
Lisp and whimper like dead men.
It's up to us to chronicle
Their thoughts, that death not treat them all
The way that life did, flat forgetful.

Fred

What a swarm of stories there
Must be, to overload the air
With voices as loud as a river's roar.

Reynolds

The number, of course, is infinite.

Fred

Why couldn't a single story tell it
All?

Reynolds

Ah, that's the helpless poet
In you, the need to generalize
From yours to all men's destinies.
For fiction, those are pompous lies
Which try to stretch the single stories
Into laws akin to physical laws.

Fred

You're no one to talk. *A Long
And Happy Life* will make as strong
An example as any poet's song.
What is it but the ancient tale
Of Cupid and muddled Psyche? All
That's added is the motorcycle.

Reynolds

That's not the way I see it. These
Are Warren County sweethearts whose
Lives shape local clarities.

Fred

Suppose, though, that I choose to read
The myth within it. Is it so bad
To add more meaning to each word?

Reynolds

But do you add or take away?
A certain lake, a certain tree,
A particular girl on a certain day—
A fleeting tang in Carolina . . .
You'd give that up for some diviner
Heavy symbol?

Fred

But if I find a
Paradigm as old as fiction
Itself conformably mixed in?

Reynolds

Well, that requires some hard reflection.
If you think it's there it's there,
I guess. It could be anywhere,
Or not at all. *Things as they are:*
That's the novelist's true belief.
I regard the "symbol" as a thief
Which steals the best parts of a life.

Fred

I think I don't believe you quite.

Reynolds

I'm overstating it a bit
To make my point. Jim Applewhite
Would have conniptions if he were here—

Fred

And Spender too.

Reynolds

Things as they are:
I'll stand by what I see and hear.

Fred

And does that mean the poet's blind
And deaf? Let's say he's trained his mind
To hear all, multivoiced as wind.

Reynolds

Wind's what the poet cannot fix;
The current of life from Eden to Styx
Demands an accounting of *the facts.*
Poems are maimed by their timelessness,
Lack of distinction in *was* and *is,*
That stony stillness like a star of ice.
The *symbol* is at last inhuman,
A cruel geometry, and no man
Ever loved one like a woman
Or a novel.

Fred
Oh, come now. Yeats—

Reynolds

I except of course the crazy poets
Who can fall in love with rocks and he-goats.

(Enter Susan with tea and cakes.)

Fred

Now just a minute . . .

Susan
Boys, boys.
I'm surprised you make such a dreadful noise.
—Reynolds, your Oxonian poise!
Old Fred *never* had a grain
Of couth, but you're a *gentleman* . . .
Don't you-all hear how the wind's brought rain?

(They fall silent and listen. Susan pours.)

Fred

The most symbolic line there is,
And fullest of hard realities,
Is Shakespearean: "Exeunt omnes."

Reynolds

Your poet's a foe to love and laughter.
Here's the line one gives one's life for:
"They all lived happily ever after."

Susan

I wish I weren't a writer's wife.
I'd live as harmless as a leaf
And cuddle up in a dear warm life.

The Rain (to The Wind)

What say we work us up some brio
And drown this silly wayward trio?
My favorite line is "Ex Nihilo."

The Wind

Leave them in peace, if peace there is
For their clamorous little species;
Let them relish their flimsy wishes.
Tomorrow and tomorrow we
Advance against them frightfully.
This night at least they have their say
Together; and the force of Time
Upon their arts, upon slant rhyme
And paragraph, delays for them.
It's soon enough that we dissolve
Their names to dust, unmoving move
Against their animal powers to love
And weep and fear. It's all too soon
They grow as silent as the moon
And lie in earth as naked bone.
We'll let them sit and sip their tea
Till midnight; then I'll shake the tree

Outside their window, and drive the sea
Upon the land, the mountain toward the Pole,
The desert upon the glacier. And all
They ever knew or hoped will fall
To ash. . . . Till then, though, let them speak
And lighten the long dim heartache,
And trifle, for sweet trifling's sake.

KELLY CHERRY

After Catullus 1

Now to whom am I going
to give this neat, new little book?
It was just this very minute prettily polished
with a dry pumice stone . . .

To you, dear Cornelius.
For you did use to find my trifling verses
of some value, even back then
when you alone among Italians grandly dared
to unfold all time in three volumes.
How learned they were! and full of labor.

So take this, friend, for yourself—
such as it is.
And on my behalf beseech the muse:

May it endure a little longer than its author.

A Bird's-Eye View of Einstein

You start from the point of perch.
                              Here, air's restless
And lambent, licking at leaves like candlelight.
Next, you hold your candle high.
                              Looking off,
You will be able to see a century
Of holocausts, smoking on the lip of space.
Go ahead and preen: Before we sing or swing,
We start from point of view.
                              Time, that flies, lights
On the optic nerve and beats its wings against
My brain. My skull's a nest socked between branch
And sky. I train my eagle eye on dark

Shadows scudding across the hemisphere.
I swoop; I lift; shadows are preyed on here.
The crop of time is choked with sigh and tear.

Concerning the First Relation: Bridegroom

Last, you listen. One cry echoes, echoes,
And echoes. It's insistent as sleet but light
As light. The skyline bats it back and forth.
Like a shuttlecock slapped out of season,
It maps a parabolic flight, and fall.
I track its arc, am cautioned, turn away,
Trim my lamp.
                        I go down before I go
Down. The hotel sign spills neon on the street
And neon stains the snow. My husband stands
With his back to the window, looking in.
His hands rest on my head, my hair towels
The snowflakes from his feet, and if I sin,
I sip salvation like sweet wine, wiping
My mouth on his thigh.
                                    Still, unquiet shadows
Ring the room, and remind me of someone
Who stalks my steps down dead-end streets and stops
If I stop and waits, patient and intent,
While I climb the stairs, use the phone, undress,
And drop off into unprotected sleep.
When the light goes out, I marry the man
Who ties my tongue, dazzles my brain, and turns
My wrists to water. He meets me under the roof
Of my mouth, where I leak profanity and store
Desire against the day of reckoning
When our hearts go hungry.
                                        I eat the Christ.
My face grows warm with work. I feel foolish
As a virgin: My spine's exposed to cold
Air and my scalp smells of sweat. I could swear
He mocks my greed and the servility

It brings me to, but spares me, from a sense
Of pity or proportion, or because
He's got better things to do than scorn
Venus for her visibility, earth
For being walked on. Forbearance makes me sick
With shame.
                    Aquila's Altair shies from sight,
But I run out into the night, spewing
This holy seed upon the waste land.

                                        O

Men and women, love according to law.
The one you covenanted with is jealous
Of your affections, and causes the child
Of adultery to curse the day he was born.
Divorce yourselves from idols. Raise your young
On the fruits of faith.
                    I weep bitterly,
Scavenging in back alleys for fly-specked scraps
And moldy crusts. I lean against the tree
That glows green-black, with a bark like opal,
Under the street lamp. Moral knowledge sucks
Up moisture from the soil of paradise.
How many trees history exacts, and how
Broken the land becomes!
                                    I rake kindling
From my unclean hair.
                                    Then the sun, burning
Up an Eddic vine, tops out, flaring up
In a brief explosion of photosynthesis
Manqué, the pinnate green gone awry, white
Hot and flashy like a tree of mirrors,
The golden bough issuing in crystal light.
At this point Phlegethon purls and spurtles
Beneath Boulevard Bridge, and overflows
The Fan, inflaming whole families with thirst
For the inconceivable. A monstrous
Appetite, glutting itself on human flesh
Gutted by fire, hankers after that still

Tougher substance speared on a stick of wood,
And seared by this savage culture.
                                    All myths
Meet and mingle here, weep, giggle and come
Sour as pulp in my mouth. Nothing is born
That dies. My mouth will hatch a skyful of
Raucous words that endure endlessly, like
Certain sound waves, retrievable, static
And irrelevant.
                    And once in Richmond
When Monument was buried under snow,
And even the General's horse seemed hewn from blue
Ice, I saw my best beloved, He of
The Black Moods, reel in his steaming breath, gulp
The windy words, grow fat and gouty, lie
Swollen beneath the slush and drift, waiting,
Helpless as an infant, for warm weather
And release from earth. Then I nailed him down
Upon that visionary rock, and sowed
Bird seed in his wounds. The gashes yielded
A fowl harvest, an ornithology
Of blood, and feathers flowered in his veins
Until he suffocated by the force
Of that green fuse that lit the landscape up
By day, and burned it out by night.
                                    I watch
Disaster feeding on the crumbs of stale
Hope. She grows up, grows fat, grows old and dies.
An eyrie cheeping crashes on the scree,
Like surf. Nestlings persist. Her fluids clot
Their down, while maggots breed in bloodied straw.
Each hungry beak will raid its brother's craw.

Concerning the Middle Term: Ghost
My brother lives in Bronxville, Belsen, Rome,
Belfast and Quebec. He has three blind wives
Who wind the clock on Sunday. See how they
Run: one to Reno, one to Richie Small.

But one's got something cooking in the oven
And it's not by Pillsbury.
                              I recall
The names and dates he wishes I'd forget.
How, feeling up my friend from school, he jabbed
His hand on a strategic safety pin;
The woman from Haiti whose hair came off in his hand
One night; and the night we said our name over
And over, while the cigarette between
His fingers smouldered and went out, and light
Held its breath an hour or two and then blew
Out the day.
                   We lay on the outer shore
Of space, cast up by a soundless solar
Wind from the depths of time. Each light wave touched
His hair with damp; I dried him with my breath.
But we grow old and grow apart. Betray
Thy brother: This is the first death. My heart
Collects vibrations like a shell, tuning
The stars' breeze to a fever pitch, and still,
When wives walk slowly round the universe
And spin the orbit of our planet out
According to their measure, I deny
I ever knew him.
                       I play hide-and-seek
In Ithaca. My brother combs the gorge.
I am seven. I wear my birthstone, pack
A pistol, and I hug my quick shadow
In secret, but my brother finds me out
Behind the evergreen.
                              Is this the tree
In Revelation 22, verse two,
Whose leaves restore the nations, and, if not,
Why did my brother carve his name and mine
In a Cupid's target, and why was this
Woody scroll unrolled in darkness, and read
Among the dying and the dead? Something
Keeps me, and keeps me looking for that lost

Word, the one which answers to the grave.

O

Bereft and saddened populations, be
Gladdened by light, and channel light downward
To earth, and let it wash the flesh away
From these dry bones, that the hand of the Lord
May gentle them, and move the slow marrow
To praise and a beginning.

When we raise
Our eyes and fling them out like stones, rippling
The surface of the Milky Way, we look
Backward in time. My brother used to dive
For motes. They float among the atoms, scarce
As pearls, and each pearl plucked will buy the eye
Of a needle. Then he drowned. And now I skim
Galactic shallows, looking for the one
Husband of my sightless sisters. I glide
Along the currents of Andromeda,
Because my brother's body, unfathomed
For two million years, preceding Perseus,
Lies broken on the reef, locked in a cold
Luminescence.

I see the whitened bones,
Scoured as though by salt, drifting aimlessly
Like driftwood, from world to world in an ocean
Of light. What nebula, what nebula
Irrigates the shrubs of heaven!

At this
Point Phlegethon charts a new course, cresting
On a hillside outside home. I feed fish
Of fire to orphans. Still they beg for more.
Give them more: This was my brother's body,
With which he warmed my own. All night we crouched
Side by side, holding hands, while bombs splintered
The sky into slivers of light, and one
Spark lodged deep in his windpipe, fatal as
An arrow dipped in venom, and I sucked

The poison out, but silence told me he
Was gone away, wedded to the woman
I was not.
                    I see disaster brooding
Over the past. Her wide and nervous wings
Eclipse the echoing moon, but soon the sun
Startles her into flight. Not until night
Does she return, bringing burning and old
Mad grief for the fatherless and unborn.

Part Three: Infinity
Our father moves among his many rooms.
Silent as light, he builds and blueprints, both
At once, in the single act of passing
Through. His house is walled with light. The window
Gives onto a lawn of light stretching in all
Directions back onto itself. I find
My view encompassed by my pupil, shrunk
Before the fact of brilliance. My tongue's gone dry
As dry ice, and my hands sweat salt water
Streams. There is a taste of ash on my teeth.
The half-moon of my thumbnail shows its dark
Side to the sun, and hangs in the branches of
My body. My blood glows, and flows uphill—
And still I'm circumscribed by being, fenced
In by myself. My father locks the door
And throws the key away.
                                        Here is the room
Where the music is made.
                                        Here is the room
Where violins are played, and light is made
Of light, and sound falls to the ground like fruit
Shaken from a full tree.
                                        Here is the room
Where sound is splayed into chromatic scales.
Here is the room where violins are played.
I listen on my back; my father counts

The measured rests strewn freely and with glee
Down the page, like centers of gravity,
Equilibrating energy.
                                        I am
That discordant note which calls attention
To itself. My soul fidgets and rasps. I cough.
My creating father doesn't care how
Tightly music clasps my hand, how violent
Are the strokes his rosined bow has drawn across
My neck, nor what lesser pulse keeps time there,
Nor does he hear how wonderfully well I wail
In harmony.
                        I skulk in corners crammed
With old resentment. I chew sugar cane
In Baton Rouge, and I search the scorched fields
For my father, but he lies hidden in
The earth, asleep and dreaming of the day
When sunlight sloshing on his face will wake
Him up to play duets with Einstein.
His artful innocence has undone mine.
If I find him, I'll flush him out and plant
Cold kisses on his forehead for a sign.
The cross I work to snare him with is made
Of peat moss, and it smells of bitter smoke.
I lurk behind the blind and bring down birds
Of peace. Such small and airy skeletons
Sizzle in the Lake of Fire, and sink!
                                        O
Children of judgment, choose goodness. Banish
Arbitrary hurt, but know that the root
Wrenched from dry ground weeps gravel and requires
Righting, or all the oppressed land will groan
Under blanching stocks and sharp, sunburned rocks
Will bruise and singe your soles.
                                        My father slips
Through tall sweetness.
                                        Instantly, Phlegethon
Leaps to the surface, spilling drops of flame

On Golgotha. Someone dozes on the bank
And baits his line from a can of skulls, fishing
For martyrs. I reel in my breath, and steal
Past poetry, to where my father waits
With sad expectancy in his eyes; I think
He knows how much he wronged me when he went
Away, but I am as implacable
As death, and just as difficult to please.
I strap him down upon the cross and skew
His skinned knees skyward. I lap lightstruck nails
Under my tongue, and spit them out one by
One. My hammer drives holes into the hands
That never touched me but only ideal
And melody, and I caress the knobs
Of his ankles, before I splice the flesh.
I soothe the tensing veins with vinegar.
I give him vinegar to drink, and sponge his brow
With vinegar, and now darkness slams down
Over the earth, like space foreclosing on
Itself, and ominous comets contract
To points without dimension, swallowing
Their toxic streams, and stars are pinched out in
That split second between dread and despair
When we become aware of God, and know
That he is absent. Thunder claps our dumb
Eyes shut, and lashes the lids with hailstones,
And earthquake heaves stony tombs up like puke.
Cry woe.
        I will split his side in two.
                            Blood
Explodes.
        I will wreak vengeance on the one
Who refused my sex.
                Cry woe.
                        I will blast
Him like an atom bomb, and crawl into
The crater of his corpse. Lymph and mucus
Are contaminated.

Cry woe.
I crawl
Into the hollow in his side, and place
My head against his heart. As unresponsive
As a desert to the changing seasons,
He suffers my cheek. When I whisper, no one
Replies, and nothing blinks or sighs or moves,
Except the wind, worming its way through bone
And carrion.
Down all the blown chambers
Of his ruining body, my cry echoes:
Why hast thou forsaken me?
Disaster
Picks the brainpan clean. Memory spatters
Darksome plumage, imagination sticks
In the flexed craw, and sense is vexed by sense.
Now is the hour. Now is the hour of woe.
I will flood the forbidden zone with tears
And rain tears on his viscera, and tears
Will run in his veins, pooling among the parched
Platelets.
The trunk takes root.
The shot limbs stir,
And light and sound swell and ripen like small
Round mustard seeds which grow into the kingdom
Of heaven, and bear faith.
Birds of the air
Stuff their nests with sinew, and make their nests
In the drafty sockets.
Now is the hour
Of closure.
Now is the hour of reprise.
Now is
The hour of recapitulation.
Time
Sings in the tree.

ITHACA

I remember a hall of doors
opening and closing. Goldfish
nibbled grainy bits in a glass bowl,
and sunlight stained the walls and floor
like finger paint. I remember
the silence, thick and spongy as bread,
and sound cutting through it like a knife.
Oh, I remember my life then, how
my parents played their violins
half the night, rehearsing, while snow
piled on the sill outside the pane.
Mike was making a model plane;
the baby slept, sucking her thumb.
I used to come home from school late—
detained for misbehavior, or
lost in a reverie on State
Street: *I, Odysseus, having dared*
to hear the sirens' song, my ears
unstopped, have sailed to Ithaca,
where the past survives. Last of all,
I remember dressing for school;
it was still dark outside, but when
the sun rose, it melted the snow.
My galoshes had small brass clasps.

HISTORY

It is what, to tell the truth, you sometimes feel
That you have had enough of, though of course
You do not really mean that, since you recall
It well enough to know things could be worse
And probably are going to get that way,
But still want a long and memorable life, which means

Having to learn more of it day by day,
The names and dates of all the kings and queens
And those less famous who ruled the territory
Known as your heart and now are gone, by one
Dark route or another, from the plot of your story.
But you write on, and are your own best Gibbon,
>   And read on, this monumental subject being
>   The decline and fall of almost everything.

Lines Written on the Eve of a Birthday

It is the loss of possibility
That claims you bit by bit. They take away
Your man, the children you had hoped would be,
They even take brown hair and give you gray
Instead. You ask if you can save your face
But that is part of their plan—to strip you
Of your future and put the past in its place.
They don't stop there. They take the skies' deep blue
And drain it off; the empty bowl they leave
Inverted, white as bone. They dust the trees
With strontium, but they keep up their sleeve
The biggest trick of all, the one that sees
>   You give up in the end. It is the loss
>   Of possibility that murders us.

Memory

These great trees, like towering sad angels,
Feathery arms flung outward and down in a stasis of despair.
This stillness of spruces.
This silence.

Like death. Like the enormous absence
That is history, a chronology
That contradicts itself.

Yes, that's right. And just think of the ones you have
Forgotten, the substitute teacher
In fourth grade, the friend who was briefly yours
Before you betrayed her, or she you.

And the one, that man,
You went walking with,
In woods outside Riga,
The green cloud of trees
In the distance, unmoving,
Embalmed in memory, if remembered at all.

If not, he was never there.
You were never in that complicated country.
You never saw how the light persevered,
Braving its way through massed branches of spruce, birch, and pine
To shine like a lantern, showing

The long way back.

A SONG

How he loved me! trembled,
        if I touched his hand.
        I saw his quick eyes glittering
        in the night.
        I saw him strip off his skin.
And white bones clattering,
        he fled into the night.

Blue Air

Against the blue air,
    He floats muter than a ghost.
I watch his wavering there,
    Upon the air,

And wait for his words to fall
    On me, words I want most.
But he says nothing at all,
    But floats above the air.

Reading, Dreaming, Hiding

> You asked me what is the good
> of reading the Gospels in Greek.
> —Czeslaw Milosz, "Readings"

You were reading. I was dreaming
The color blue. The wind was hiding
In the trees and rain was streaming
Down the window, full of darkness.

Rain was dreaming in the trees. You
Were full of darkness. The wind was streaming
Down the window, the color blue.
I was reading and hiding.

The wind was full of darkness and rain
Was streaming in the trees and down the window.
The color blue was full of darkness, dreaming
In the wind and trees. I was reading you.

LATE AFTERNOON
AT THE ARBORETUM

> Riding along in my automobile,
> My baby beside me at the wheel . . .
> —Chuck Berry

The lilacs are in bloom
and the lake that was ice
is water green as crème
de menthe. Flowering Scotch broom

tugs at the eye, Yellow
Brick Road–style. I hold
your hand; your hands, the wheel . . .
Are we saying hello,

good-bye, something in between?
The car is a Pontiac
station wagon; it's parked
in a very pastoral scene,

and as the sun enflames
the flowers, and the sky
above the arboretum
flares, then dims, making the names

of the trees difficult
to read, I study your face
in profile, now thinking
what dear Ruth had said, exult-

ing in her conscience, to
Naomi: Wherever
you go, I will come along.
    Here amid the alien heather
    and words from an old song,
I say her words, to you.

AND THERE IS FREEDOM OF A KIND
EVEN IN MERE MAGNITUDE

I shall praise his bulk,
the cave of his chest
in which I have my rest

while wearisome worries skulk
like outlaws along the perimeter
of the bed where my feet are

protected by the sheer hulk
of him. No anxiety can scale
this mountain of a male

or find me out when I flee
to sexual sanctuary!
Safe by virtue of his arms,
I set aside the old alarms
(my feminine charms).

GRAMMAIRE GÉNÉRALE: A REVIEW

> The study of the universal conditions that prescribe the form of
> any human language is "grammaire générale." Such universal
> conditions . . . provide the organizing principles that make
> language learning possible. . . . By attributing such principles
> to the mind, as an innate property, it becomes possible to
> account for the quite obvious fact that the speaker of a
> language knows a great deal that he has not learned.
> —Noam Chomsky, *Cartesian Linguistics*

for J. F.

Ten years later, I still remember the way
Your mouth on mine could make me say

Words I didn't know I knew.
Even my legs learned a new
Language. Then, speaking in tongues, I spoke with my tongue.
(I could have parsed you all night long.)

Thus love is a predicate, making sense
Of its subject even in the past tense.
Thus we conjugated, and our parts
Of speech burst into song,
As did our innocent hearts.
(I could have parsed you all night long.)

I remember how your hand translated time
Into eternity. Alas, what scans won't always rhyme:
Between *a priori* and *ex post facto,* language
Falls silent, and lovers age.
I remember what we said when we were young.
(I could have parsed you all night long.)

Love is a verb, bringing one object to bear
Upon another. It modifies fear.
Lord, we were brave and gerundive, giving
Ourselves to each other. Language is for the living;
Love is a diphthong.
(I could have parsed you all night long.)

Ten years later, I remember your mouth
On mine, its sweetness inflected with the South.
Fluent in love, you affixed your root to my prefix.
(We used adverbs for kicks.)
That night, we taught each other what we'd known all along.
(And I could have parsed you all night long.)

That night, words became hands and held each other.
Words became bodies and whispered touches, conversing with collar-
Bone, elbow and knee. Love is the mother
Tongue; you were a born scholar

And you taught me all the right ways to go wrong.
(And your dangling participle was so well hung.)

(I could have parsed you all night long.)

THE PINES WITHOUT PEER

The pines without peer
Are taller than air.

They grow in the sky,
Their roots in your eye.

And the tops of the pines wave
From the top of the sky, brave

As banners. And the tops
Of the pines are steps

To the high, wheeling
Stars. And your brain is reeling

And the trees are falling,
And you are falling

In a forest, pulled,
Drawn, blinded and mauled,

And you are the ground
And the wound

And the one wild sound.

I WILL CUT OUT MY HEART

I will cut out my heart
It has tricked me into desire
Betrayed its body and myself
Been a liar

I will cut out my heart
It has urged me to hope
Leapt like spring and stolen
The end of my rope

For this one last time
I will cut out my heart
It has bound me to love
And pulled me apart

LADY MACBETH ON THE PSYCH WARD

Doctor, I'm lost in these mazy halls that lead nowhere,
Sleepwalking through somebody else's nightmare
On Six North, wiping my hands on my hair.

There's blood on my hands, blood in my hair,
Blood between my pale scissoring legs where
It pools in my underpants—the fancy pair

I bought for him to watch me wear and not wear.
There is blood everywhere
And I am lost in it. Doctor, I breathe blood, not air.

Adult Ed. 101: Basic Home Repair for Single Women

The Tool Box
should contain utility knife
trouble light
curved-claw hammer
wrench
and rib-joint pliers.

A little putty helps.

Hacksaw and coping saw (coping saw!)
caulking gun
screwdrivers (with orange juice)—

Don't forget those rib-joint pliers.

The Power Drill
is a prerequisite for almost anything
you may wish to do: hang curtains,
pictures of your last lover,
your last lover.

Some Nails
Common ones have a large head, thick shaft. Good for the
widest variety of purposes. Box nails are thinner and may be
used where the common nail would cause splits. Roofing
nails have an extra large head and barbed shaft. The spiral
shank of the screw-nail gives it a tenacious grip. Duplex nails
are temporary. Do not expect a duplex nail to hold
permanently. This is a mistake many women make.

Types of Screws
The two universal slot designs are the straight slot and the
Phillips. Both are available in most types of screws. Look for
bright steel, dipped, galvanized, brass- or chrome-plated and
solid brass screws. Stainless steel screws are also made but they
are not always easy to find.

From time to time, you may have to call in a professional.

Painting the Ceiling
Wear goggles and mask when painting the ceiling
or going anywhere your ex-lover may be seen with his new wife.
A roller with a splash shield is also good,
whether you paint with latex
or heart's blood.

Drywall
Studs should be sixteen inches apart
but are often fewer and farther between
and let's face it, you may have seen your last stud.
In that case, use an anchor
in plaster or drywall
and repair minor cracks
by filling the voids.
Feather each coat of spackle into the surrounding area
to help hide the seam.
Soon the surface will be flawless.

Plumbing
The shit goes down the drain.

Class Commencement
Now you can begin
to put your house in order:
caulk your windows against incoming drafts,
drain outside faucets, dig up bulbs.
Prepare your bed.
Clouds are blowing in from the west, over the lake.
Winter is on its way.

Ladies, you are about to find out
just how much really rough
weather
your house can take.

She Remembers the Tears

She remembers the tears
the sun drew from her
on a hot day, the way
panic strikes and sears
the soul, a small puff
of smoke, but enough

so it disappears:
a smudge of ash
on a round stone, and none
where she used to weep tears.
The burned-out ravine
is serene.

A Scientific Expedition
in Siberia, 1913

From the log

Week One: our expedition slowed,
     Faltered, stopped; we set up
Camp and dug in, but still it snowed
     And snowed, without letup,

Until we thought we'd go insane.
     We literally lost our sense
Of balance, because sky and plain
     Were one omnipresence,

So dazzling white it could blind a man
     Or mesmerize his soul.
We lost sight of the horizon.
     There was one man, a Pole

Named Szymanowski, an expert on plants
        Of the early Pleistocene
Period, who dreamed of giants
        In the earth, swearing he'd seen

Them grow from snow like plants from dirt.
        We said that such dreams were
The price one pays for being expert,
        And laughed, but still he swore,

And still it snowed. The second week
        The ceaseless rush of wind
Was in our heads like ancient Greek,
        A curse upon our kind,

Or say: in our skulls like the drone
        Of bees swarming in a hive.
And we began to know that none,
        Or few, of us would survive.

Secretly, we sought the first signs
        Of sickness in each other,
Reading between the face's lines
        As a spy reads a letter,

But no one complained of fever,
        And suddenly the snow
Quit. You couldn't have proved it ever
        Fell, but for the wild show

Of evidence on the ground. Now
        The lid was lifted, and
Sun set icicled trees aglow
        With flame, a blue sky spanned

The hemisphere, and while we packed
        Our gear, we found we were

Singing, but Szymanowski backed
      Out, silent as the fur

On a fox . . . or the wolfish cur,
      Slinking like a shadow,
That stuck to our pack dogs like a burr.
      Where S. went, God may know,

But we went on to a frozen hill,
      A vast block of the past—
An ice cube for a drink in hell
      (If anything cools that thirst).

Inside, preserved like a foetus
      In formaldehyde, like
Life itself, staring back at us
      The mammoth creature struck

Poses for our cameras; then
      We got busy, and went
To work, and all seemed well for ten
      Days, and then some strange scent,

Not unpleasant, weighted the air,
      Sweet as fruit, and one dog
Stirred, and then another, and where
      I sat, keeping this log,

A steady dripping started up,
      Slowly at first, and then
Faster. I made my palms a cup
      To catch the flow, and when

I lapped the melted snow, I glanced
      Down, and saw how cold
Ground under my boot moved and danced
      In little streams: an old

Fear shook me and I ran to where
        The mammoth stood—freed from
Time and vulnerable to air.
        His curling tusks seemed some

Incredible extravagance,
        A creator's last spree.
His fixed stare held me in a trance,
        His reddish brown, shaggy

Coat caught the sun like burnished oak,
        But he didn't move: was still
As if he'd been carved from a rock.
        Nothing supernatural

Was going to happen, and I breathed—
        Fresh meat on the hoof!—In
An instant, the pack dogs had covered
        Him like hungry ants spreading

Over a hatching egg, tearing
        Chunks of raw flesh from his side,
Snarling, snapping their jaws, baring
        Fangs that ripped his flank wide

Open. My hands, my boots were spattered
        With blood, and the dogs ate
Him up. That horror performed, we scattered
        Into the world, but late

In the afternoon, I saw a shadow
        At my heel, and I knew
The others were dead—numbed into slow
        Motion, and each a statue

Buried in ice. And then the clouds,
        Piled in the north and east

Like a funeral parlor's stack of shrouds,
    Darkened, sliding southwest,

And it snowed and has never stopped
    Snowing since, and I have
Come with blood in my mouth, my hands sopped
    With red snow, to speak and save.

For my father,
in memoriam

The Rose

A botanical lecture

It's the cup of blood,
the dark drink lovers sip,
the secret food

It's the pulse and elation
of girls on their birthdays,
it's good-byes at the railroad station

It's the murmur of rain,
the blink of daylight
in a still garden, the clink
of crystal; later, the train

pulling out, the white cloth,
apples, pears, and champagne—
good-bye! good-bye!
We'll weep petals, and dry
our tears with thorns

A steep country springs up beyond
the window, with a sky like a pond,

a flood. It's a rush
of bright horror, a burning bush,
night's heart,
the living side of the holy rood

It's the whisper of grace in the martyrs' wood

After Catullus 85

I both hate and love. And you think I can provide
    The reason I suffer myself to be torn two ways!
I only know that in my bones I feel *I* raise
    This cross on which I'm crucified!

Love

In the attention it pays to each detail,
In its frailty and flexibility,
In the way it seeks out a new trail
While stumbling repeatedly upon the old,

You will know love, and know
That what it cannot fail to do
Is render even this late scene
In all its abundance,

The red-tailed hawk overhead,
Spongy moss springing from wet bark,
The sound of your own walking
Through these autumnal woods.

WORK

The old dog, Work, one eye blind as if seeing
wore it out, a limp in his hindquarters,
lies on his stomach on the floor at your slippered feet,
content merely to dream in your presence.

In his old age, the fur on his paws has grown
so long he, too, seems to have on slippers.
When you reach down to rub his wary ears,
he sends you a secret message of gratitude.

Strange to be here so idly, after the days
of long walks, of chasing squirrels and sticks.
The days of hunting down reluctant quarry.
There were many days when he was your one companion.

It is you who should thank him, and so you do,
inwardly. His eyes as they look up at you
are unspoken words; the blind one surely says
love. He rests his muzzle on his paws.

It may snow tonight. The storm windows
muffle the racket of the semis as they speed
past your house toward Illinois; the fire in
the fireplace makes a warm spot on the dog's coat,

you are warmed by both the fire and your dog
while candles burn and the coffee kettle heats.
It is as if your whole house is on fire
with a fire that does not burn or hurt.

This is home, where you and your old dog, Work,
hang out together, especially in autumn,
when the late tomatoes are killed by frost
and smoke from your chimney spirals into night.

GOLGOTHA

And when they were come unto a place called Golgotha, that is
to say, a place of a skull . . .
—Matthew 27:33

"Et uenerunt in locum qui dicitur Golgotha, quod est Caluariae
locus." . . . Ex quo apparet Caluariae . . . locum significare
decollatorum, ut ubi abundauit peccatum superabundet gratia
["And they came to a place called Golgotha, where Calvary is."
. . . Therefore the name of Calvary appears . . . to signify "a place
of the decapitated," so that where sin has abounded grace may
be superabundant].
—Jerome, *Commentary on St. Matthew*

They were scattered on the hillside like stones,
polished by the wind-rag: the smooth, shining bones,
cheekbone and eye socket, the empty skull-cases

of brains that had vanished into various gullets, leaving no traces
of thought, not even a single, stray
idea. For much of that long, painful day

he must have contemplated the meanings of
erosion, mortal decay, vanity, impermanence, rather than love,
until in the lengthening light

that drew on toward—but he would never see it—that night,
he saw—a trick of his blood-blurred eyes, perhaps—them move,
and knew the meaning of the skulls was love

and knew the one proposition needing no proof
is that God exists because God thinks or is thought of.
God is what remains in the final analysis.

And Then

And then a vast, surprising peacefulness
descended, like a blue shadow upon
the snow; and the shadow sleeping on the snow
was a kind of reconciliation, form
embraced by content, light by light, the birds
hanging from the branches like bright red berries.

And then for days, there was nothing to disturb
the beauty of that equilibrium,
which was so like the miracle of forgiveness.

R. H. W. Dillard

Why Were the Bandit's Eyes Hidden behind a Green Mask?

The stuttering bishop,
The midwife,
And there were the children
Strung across the highway
Like Christmas festoons.

The carriage was of gold
And gleamed,
And the peasants bore rakes
To ravish the ladies.
(That year was a time.)
The leaves fell early.

The dust day low.

The horse's ears were back,
His beribboned tail,
The pinwheels of his eyes,
The foam,
His teeth were flat and wide,
And the bridge we never reached.

On Mynydd Hiraethog: Afternoon

for Ian and Kanta Walker

On Mynydd Hiraethog high near Llyn Alwen
Where the hill peels off from the stone tower
And the stained glass creaks in the dark house,
The wind cracks the air as you would crack an egg,
Splits and separates it, lays the flat grass flatter
And makes a man lean heavy, angle out.
The rain comes in level, and you must turn

The top of your cap into it like a round tweed shield.
The windscreen wipers of your car slip through,
Only lead you blind to the edge of the road
And the moor sliding off under the gravel.
Denbigh Castle was in friendly hands, safe
With wide boards laid on the damp shirred stone,
And the Vale of Llangollen will be still
With chimney smoke hanging low and steady,
But on Mynydd Hiraethog the storm
Stirs Llyn Alwen into stiff froth,
Winds the dim hallways of the stone house
Shrill with the afternoon, whips clouds
Into flat rain, and forces you to faith,
Leaning down to sunset on the wind.

Meditation for a Pickle Suite

Morning: the soft release
As you open a jar of pickles.
The sun through the window warm
And moving like light through brine,
The shadows of pickles swim the floor.
And in the tree, flowing down the chimney,
The songs of fresh birds clean as pickles.
Memories float through the day
Like pickles, perhaps sweet gherkins.
The past rises and falls
Like curious pickles in dark jars,
Your hands sure as pickles,
Opening dreams like albums,
Pale Polish pickles.
Your eyes grow sharp as pickles,
Thoughts as green, as shining
As rows of pickles, damp and fresh,
Placed out in the afternoon sun.

CONSTRUCTION

It seems that the human mind has first to construct forms
independently before we can find them in things.
—Albert Einstein

Vladimir Tatlin's demand:
Real materials in real space,

Solid and silent, an art of iron,
Of concrete, cut wood and glass.

A response: to say as you see,
Words set firm like a jaw.

The descent into silence. An ascent.
You breathe as you sleep, you circulate.

To say as you see. To see as by stop-action,
Clouds coil overhead, the passage of days,

Trees bend by the side of the road
Like tires on a curve, plants uncurl,

How the world dissolves in the water of the eye:
The illusion speed produces. The reality of speed.

A result: to see as you say,
As gravity may bend a ray of light.

To say the earth's center is of fire:
Life leaps from the soil like sun flares.

To see the world made true,
An art of rocks and stones and trees,

Real materials in real space,
L'esthétique de la vitesse.

March Again

> The stable universe is slipping
> away from under us.
> —Alfred North Whitehead

How the light returns to you,
How even the gray bark of trees
Seems to shed light and the ground
Is as bright and as fluid as air.
How your skin opens like an eye:
You are warm as glass, as clear.

In the evening it snows
And the wind rattles the roof
Like knuckles or bullets,
The curtains puff away
From the closed windows.
You hold to the lamp's circle,
Well away from the wall.
Only blood moves through you
Like light through fog,
You close your eyes
And the room silently moves.

In the morning the wind sharpens
The pond to blades, to light,
Wave on wave on wave.
You grow dizzy and each step
Is like walking on water,
Is like walking on knives.
The wind is around you like a wall.

How you are stirring like a bulb
In soil, you open like an eye,
The lids curled back like lips
In a snarl, how you follow

The shadows of birds, a tatter
As of discarded paper or shavings,
How the day stretches like dogs
And the shadows shrink in the grass.

Christ could have swum away
From the cross on air,
But he chose to be nailed
To the ground. You grow dizzy
And each step is like walking
On water, is like walking on knives.
The ground sheds light like a lamp.
The wind rattles the trees like bones.
Only blood calls you to move
Well away from the walls.

GETTYSBURG

It don't hurt a bit to be shot in a wooden leg.
—Lt. Gen. Richard S. Ewell, CSA

for Bruce and Betsy Stefany

It is a swelling and falling away of ground,
Stones and stone, the trees lined up along the wall,
And an accumulation of names.

Gettysburg has an echo
Like a shout in rocks.
You hear it
Even when you look away.

Say Spangler's Spring or Culp's Hill,
The Round Tops, the Angle,
Say the Devil's Den,
Say Cemetery Hill.

Fifty thousand hit in July,
Down in Pennsylvania farm dirt.
Richard Dillard felt his leg collapse
With a bright stain like a fallen flag.
Home is just over the hill, they said,
And two years later it was.

We'll fight them, sir, till hell freezes over,
And then, sir, we'll fight them on the ice.

Too bad, Lee said, too bad.
Oh, too bad. And then the rain
Slid down the butts of rifles,
Down the barrels and bayonet blades
And into the ground, the first drops
Dancing in the dust like live things,
Then a rush that laid all dust to rest.

The real war was somewhere to the west.
This one was only a dream, a spring
Of dreams, dreams that still splash
Like living things on the ground.

It is ground and grass,
A piling up of names like stones,
It is earth and air, a place to live.
You can move through echoes without a glance
Or drop them like postcards into the box
To be sent on with best wishes.

Or you can walk out Wainwright Avenue,
Past Hancock on his horse, and Slocum,
Slowly, thinking of another day, other days,
Watch the high clouds circle like birds
And hold hands or not this day, as you will.

You feel the muscles in your legs
Climbing Culp's Hill, climbing the tower

On Culp's Hill, feel the blood moving
In them like slow ice or warm as plowed ground.
Names fade in this accumulation of air.
You can see the day turn through the clouds.

If you need to remember anything,
It is the best way home.

TALKING TO TREES

> "They seem to have very good manners.
> Do they never speak?"
> —Robert Louis Stevenson

Sun stained and sun showered,
You are standing in high trees
Watching the sunlight shiver down
With the afternoon's warm rain.

The trees are speaking in leaf patter,
The patois of leaf and sprinkled water,
Whisper and whisper, semaphore of light
And the air's twisting reply.

This is the language of light,
Of water and air, earth speaking
In wet bark and the wide spreading
Of leaves, the tap and tussle of leaves.

You are alone in the woods
And you are talking to trees,
The sibilance of sycamores,
Sumac's silence and the oak's high rattle.

The vines wrinkle and turn underfoot,
Jewelweed springing in your fingers

And flicking the small brown seeds
Between wide roots of the balsam fir.

Dots of mud on the woodland floor,
Needled and notched, the scattered trunk
Of a fallen walnut, dissolving back to soil,
And high above, the clinging mistletoe.

They are speaking weather words
And words beyond weather, stone's slow decay,
Root's press into the layered ground,
Water's rise to greet the sun in green.

You are word-bound and tongue-tied,
Shy in the hushing of trees,
But you say what you have come to say,
"Tree," as you touch bark shyly, "Trees."

The light rain passes soon,
Leaving the sun cracks in the mealy earth
Beyond the trees unsoothed, sun scorched,
Meadow and dry creek bed, dying wind.

You are talking to trees
And you are not alone,
Standing in the catalpa's shadow,
Hearing earth's answer in trees.

What to Do (When You Want to Say So Much and You Do Not Know How)

You are far away,
Space dipping and swaying in time,
And I have something to say
But do not know just how.

If I could speak in light
(Eight and a half minutes from sun to earth)
I would, words on solar wind,
Lighting up the polar sky,
Curtains curving,
Rivers of noun and verb.

One word will do,
Or two, or more,
But if no words will come:

Try flowers,
Rosemary for remembrance,
Myrtle for love, the humble hyssop,
Hyacinth for peace of mind,
The discreet daisy that will not tell,
Light from the buttercup that dares tell all,
The complex history of the rose,
Messenger at the door, puzzle and surprise.

Or other symbols,
Rat's evil, snake's sly appeal,
Rabbit's belief, watchful rooster,
Lazy cat, pelican's care,
Cross and double cross, hammer and star,
River and still water, mountain too high
To cross, planet in the evening sky,
The good man's strawberry, true fish,
Rainbow of promise, pot of fool's gold,
Sun's simple code of dark and light.

Codes,
The cleverness of codes,
The stammer and hiccup of electronic dot and dash,
Or the older rhythms of the telegrapher's fist,
Smoke signals from a nearby hill,
The innocent page covered with invisible ink
(You hold it to the fire),

Lines at the end of the letter—

     xxx

     ooo

Or blocks of inscrutable letters—

VZIVZ SPNHW IOPQW VZIVZ SPNHW IHLKV
ZIVZS PNHWI HIAYQ FVZSP OLPYP IJIUH
LKVZI VZSPN HWIUI LAAKO PQW

Try other languages,
Unfamiliar words,
Clicks and glottal stops,
Sounds of the palate, sounds of the nose,
Gujarti, Wendish or Dard,
Luvian, Lydian, Lycian,
Pashto or Kurdish,
Loops and curls of Arabic,
Strokes and bars of Chinese,
Pig Latin, Hog Latin
(Osay uchmay, osay uchmay),
So you may say it and be heard
But not be heard too soon,
The dictionary as go-between,
John Alden kneeling on the floor
Leafing back and forth from page to page to page.

Or other languages,
The language of the dog,
Cocked head, the wagging tail,
Hackles brisk along the spine,
The wow-wow-wow, wouah, wouah,
Dance of the empty dinner bowl
Across the kitchen's linoleum floor.

Language of the cat
(Fifteen words have been catalogued)
Or of the jackdaw

(Kia, kiaw, fly away, fly back,
Perhaps the only words I need,
Kiaw, kiaw),
Seven words of the rooster
In the chickenyard,
Typed letters of the kitten on the keys,
ew 31pol;,
The language ('Attar told us) of the birds
Who sought the Simurgh
And found the Simurgh to be themselves.

Tintin talking to the elephants,
Sol-lah-te-doh and doh-te-lah-sol,
Or Tarzan's notes on Pal-ul-don:
Otho, God's name,
A-ul-as, light of the sun,
Otho-sog-as, eclipse,
And you—Lo, Ro, A-ul-un.

Language of the telegraph vine,
Moth's scent, bee's dance,
Antennae of the ants, quiver and touch,
The thunderhead's announcement in advance,
Trees' leaves that dimple in the wind,
Bits along the DNA, neutrino's whiz,
The quark's surprise.

The poetry of penguins
(Read Le Guin), the poetry of stones,
The poetry of planets
Singing into silent space,
Curving time.

Or the language of dreams,
Freud's comic signs,
Scaling the building's wall,
Snake in the grass,
Hat of a man, stairways and shafts,

Persons in a landscape,
Narrow narrow streets,
Causeways,
And other dreams,
Mountains, rivers,
Writing on the walls,
City landscape and the duck's escape,
Your face,
And when I said so much.

Or if I have the words
(I think I do),
Perhaps the medium is at fault,
Try others:
Tomtom in the jungle's dark,
Code of the radio, the telegraph,
Vibrations on a string between tin cans,
Chalk carvings on a mountainside,
A small box in the classifieds,
Billboard by the road,
Or just a postcard with boxes to check:
[   ] Having wonderful time
[   ] Wish you were here
[   ] Don't forget to feed the canary
[   ] My window is the one with the X
[   ] Hello hello hello
[   ] So much

Or wig-wag, semaphore:

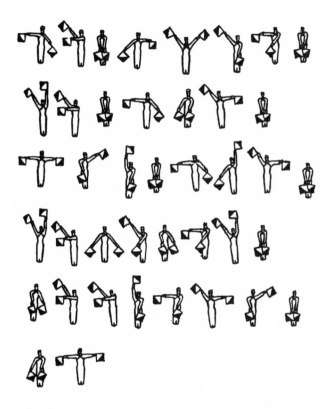

Or if you are not so really far away
And we are face to face,
A wink, a nod, turn of the head,
Firm handshake, swift embrace,
Language of the wrinkled brow,
Lip's turn, of legs, of fingers,
Familiar language of the eyes,
Or simply say the thought
That comes to mind,
Or think that thought
And it will then be said.

Messages,
The message of the dawn,
Orange dusk,
Message curling on the wind,
Pigeon's wing, mosquito's hum,

Message that washes through your nerves like water
When something dark blacks out the stars
And passes, lets them shine again,
Message that flutters on solar wind
To which we all respond,
You and I and rocks and stones and trees,
The message I will not say,
Message you will not say,
Message we both will hear.

Or, say, silence. . . .
Silence that says so much. . . .
Silence that says. . . .
And says. . . .

THE GREETING

Hello. It is like an echo
Of something I have always known:
From a bush (where you are burning),
From a cloud (you are alone),
The stream's dry whisper, river's slide,
Stone, thistle, the startling leap
Of a jewel weed. I always know the voice.
It is one day hers; one day, his.
Today it is yours.

Hello. And the leaves lapse
Into applause, a flight of monarchs
Dizzies and stills, the high stone arch
Coos with a flutter of doves.
It is like a breeze I have always felt,
Billowing out the silent curtains,
Bumping the pictures on the walls.
One day it is a warm breeze; one day, cold.
Today it is you.

Hello. It is like the face
Of someone I have always known:
The smile of recognition, frown of fear,
Snarl that splits it like a shell,
Blank face of the dreamer, silent dream.
I have always known the dream,
How it lights and flares, how it fades.
It is one day mine; one day, yours.
It is today.

21. MONTAGE: HIS PRAYER

from *January: A Screenplay*

In this cold dark house:
In this motion:
This prayer:

For my sorrow in this depth of joy,
Gift beyond reward, I'm sorry.
For the joy I feel in this broken world,
This sorrow, this woe, I thank you,
I thank you.

Prayer of the given world,
Prayer of the frozen grass,
Sheathed blade and blade and blade,
Prayer of the shattered tree,
Prayer of the rabbit in the road,
Prayer of the white crowned sparrow
Pitched stiff by the feeder, iced,
Prayer of the weed and creeping vine,
Prayer of the bent tree, twisted
And leaning, leaning and turned,
Prayer of the saw blade,
Prayer of the chisel,

Prayer of the roadsign, iced over
And glaring,
Prayer of the hand,
Prayer of the thigh,
Prayer of the eye, open and trying to see,
Prayer of the mind, confused
And thanks giving,
Prayer of the ice,
Prayer of the moving air,
Prayer of the sun, invisible
And clouded from rising to setting,
Prayer of the earth,
Prayer of the world, this motion,
This turning,
Prayer of the lover, this prayer,
Lover and lover, distant and loving,
Alone and lonely, alone in love
Fulfilled, prayer and prayers,
This prayer of thank you,
This motion of thanks,
This dark cold house of thanks.

TIPS FOR A TRAVELLER

for Julia Johnson

In the Isle of Bananas,
The Republic of Fronds, you must
Always remember to sway with the wind,
Allow rages to pass into a whisper,
Bow your head before the blast
And wait for the approach of the eye.

In the Archipelago of Sky,
The Republic of Clouds, you must
Always remember to drift with the wind,

Skirt thunderheads with their ragged
Electric feet, thin out in sunlight
And flow across the moon all night.

In the Oberland of Height,
The Republic of Peaks, you must
Always remember to climb with the wind,
Cling to cragheads and sheets of stone,
Beware treacherous snows, seek shelter
When avalanches stumble from above.

In the Bower of Love,
The Republic of Amour, you must
Always remember to become the wind,
Expect constant surprise, suffer
The days to pass like turtles, the nights
To clang into explosions like prepared pianos.

In the Delta of Lianas,
The Republic of Rain, you must
Always remember to forget the wind,
To lie still in the moisture of your skin,
To bathe in the shadows of forgotten sunlight
Across a wide expanse of silent savannas.

A DREAM OF UNCLES

I have been blessed with uncles
Who took me hunting for squirrel
And for crows, who shovelled
The stiff hound into the hole
I helped dig, who rode with me
In the bed of the truck, tilted
In a cane bottomed chair, showed
Me the rhythm of words on a page,
Let me ramble the bookshelves,

Palmed a silver dollar into my hand
For no reason other than I was there.

The wisdom of uncles, their advice
Like silver on a day crowded with crows,
Black beaks, ruffed necks, black claws,
Caws scattering the silence into shards
Of cracked glass; like silver which warms
To the touch quickly, is valuable
In exchange, shines like caught water
Catching light by desert palms.

My dead uncle Clifton who died young,
So mysterious, only a silver shadow
In an album, a headstone, and now
So many uncles dead; let me name
The living: Grant and Letcher,
Basil and George, all of them alive,
And all my uncles grinning in photographs,
Lounging against each other, shy,
Ducking their heads, ready to break free,
Move away from the Kodak's click.

Last night I dreamed of cats, the dream book
Warns of treachery in those close,
Cats playing, leaping, stretching their claws,
The black cat strikes like lightning,
But my uncles were there as well,
Predicting prosperity, Uncle Carroll
As silent and relaxed as one of his cows
Answering to her name, and Kenner, Charlie,
Wilbur well again, the boy who should
Not have lived but did, all my other uncles
In other rooms, just beyond the open door.

These are only names to you, but perhaps
You'll understand what I mean, what a dream
Of uncles really means, even if I don't

Spell it out: a gray day, nothing stirs,
The crow's black eye foretells the night,
Claws swell from the black cat's paws,
Your shoulders will not lift, betrayed,
You are ready to cry uncle, give in,
It is then that you have a dream of uncles,
A house full of uncles, uncles lolling
On the porch steps, uncles in bed,
Uncles napping on the sofa, your uncle
Passing silver over your palm, the future
In your hands, it glints like dawn,
A breeze stirs the bare branches
And crows burst into something like a song.

AUTUMN LETTER TO LONDON

Yes, Julia, London is not home, has a river,
    A great river, to be sure,
But not the Father of Waters, only a sliver,
    Not long though wide and deep
With history echoing along the barges
    And banks like the bells
Of Big Ben (the very name enlarges
    Your sense of who you are,
Of where you really are), Shakespeare
    In conversation with a boatman
Whom, on a sudden whim, he makes steer
    Back up the river to where they began,
Or Turner catching the Parliament fire
    In oil and water, or even Eliot
Dreaming of a gilded barge, a choir
    Of nymphs, a golden past
That never was in just that way.
    It was not home to them
Either, although they did manage to stay
    Longer than you plan to do.

Rumor has it you did see the Queen,
    One of the Little Princesses grown up
Who stood on the palace balcony, were seen
    There braving the bombs of the blitz.
They were the first thing about London
    I noticed, apart from Dick Whittington's cat,
Those little girls looking up and down,
    Then at the camera, waving, brave,
Ignoring the Heinkels high overhead, thick wings
    With bent noses like sharks,
Waved, smiled, were not afraid, flames licking
    At London, fooled only themselves, and us.
No, it is not home. The sun sets
    Almost before it rises.
The cold fogs rise in damp runlets
    That brush your face
Like cold scarves. Think how thick
    And dark they must have been
In coal-fired days: quite a trick
    Just to maneuver down the street,
The gas lamps just yellow blurs
    Filtered through wet wool.
I don't know why all this occurs
    To me just now. London was always
Bright and clear when I was there,
    Young women's legs sunburnt bright
Red all down the backs, like flares
    Along the streets, the fronts
Still white as winter, never thought
    To rotate in the grass
Along the Serpentine, simply sought
    The bright heat you are missing
Now. Maybe it's because it is so cold
    And gray here in Virginia
Today. Even New Orleans broke old
    Records for low temperatures
Last night. Your cat Henrietta
    Must be curled in a ball

Or maybe writing you a letter
    The way she used to do
Before the summer skittered away
    Through some hole or the other
Leaving only ice pellets that flay
    The air like a cat-o'-nine-tails.
These are autumn thoughts, winter
    In the air, counting birthdays,
Shocked at the sum, memory bent to
    New tasks, listing, numbering,
Leafing through the past like the album
    I found in my mother's attic
With pictures of the man whose thumb
    Dug into my ear and found dimes—
The Mexican magician who lived down the hall,
    Or the wrestler who tried to teach
Me how to swim, or the Florida fall
    When I started off to school
Where I've stayed ever since, kept
    From graduation by people
Like you, poets whose language leapt
    To make each day new anew.
This year at the college it's all been
    Reports and memos, meetings
That always seem to start, never end
    Until exhaustion sets in.
But no complaints from me. I'm writing
    Poems between appointments,
Teaching Hitchcock, actually delighting
    In the words writers hand
Me to read. Anita, for example, is working
    On a story about the color red,
Another about little boys who are lurking
    Everywhere you'd never think to look,
And even one about a girl who likes
    To count. What more could I ask?
The dog and I scratch fleas, take hikes
    Around the neighborhood, hoping

They'll hop off or freeze along the way;
        The cat's rough tongue seems
To do the job for her. I'd even say
        There was a lesson in that
For us all, but I don't want to believe it.
        Anyway, as I was saying, the memories
Rise in autumn, the past, if you retrieve it,
        Causing, say, you, in my dreams,
To walk on lily pads in Florida, make forays
        Across the long causeway in a jeep,
As in a story by Nabokov or maybe Borges.
        But what does this have to do with London?
Or even home? Perhaps an autumn definition
        Of just what London or Shakespeare
Or home or your cat or mine or my contrition
        At not writing you as I promised
Have in common. Even hot Mercury has ice caps,
        The newspaper noted yesterday.
Cats can be replaced by better mousetraps
        Although they'll seldom purr.
Promises are never kept in just the way
        We planned. The days do grow shorter,
And even the Mississippi, like a Shakespeare play,
        Comes to a satisfying or an ambiguous end
(You deconstruct it as you wish). Still, the
        Promises are kept—like appointments
On a busy day, breathless, willy nilly,
        With irritation or apology in haste,
But kept. If winter comes, the poet said,
        Can spring be far behind?
And sure enough a purple finch, tipped red
        Along the upper half of its body,
Just landed at my empty feeder to remind me
        That the seed is still in the cellar
And, before spring comes, I should kindly
        Keep my promise, do my job.
So, Julia, I'd better end this letter
        And get to it.

But, a reminder to you: you'd better
        Continue to look both ways
Before you cross a British street,
        Watch winter deepen every day,
Observe, and read the poems of Louis MacNeice,
        Take notice when he says,
"What the wind scatters, the wind saves."
        The wind ruffles the finch's red feathers.
I've got to go. Remember: the love that enslaves
        Us, ties us to the world in ice and fire,
Runs like a river through our days and nights
        From frigid Minnesota to the Gulf,
Wrinkles the frozen sky in fiery northern lights,
        Also ties us together, together or apart.

WINTER LETTER TO BLUEFIELD

The images, Anita, that come to mind
        When you write a letter,
Or when I write one, a rare enough event . . .
        Perhaps I'd better
Explain just what I mean, since meaning
        Is somehow what I think
This will all be about—so, what I mean
        Is just that curious mental kink
Which creates the person you're writing to
        (In this instance, you) clearly in focus
At a particular moment in time's texture
        At a single locus,
That set of all points defined by who you are—
        In your own special case
(Appropriately enough for someone who has asked
        "Who am I?" to herself, face to face)
Two images, twinned, one by actual memory,
        The other by *its* twin, imagination:
The first, memory's gift from the night
        While on a nocturnal peregrination,

Walking the dog across the campus,
    I saw you through lit window glass
Writing a story on solar radiation, oblivious
    To our presence, our shadow pass
Across your field of vision. You were wearing
    Headphones like a wandering solarnaut,
Listening, I suppose, to some kind of music
    And, whether hearing it or not,
Swaying to its rhythm as though to a spring breeze
    Or the virtual music of the spheres.
I was not spying, I assure you, no Peeping Tom
    No matter how it appears,
Just the dog and I walking by, looking in
    But knowing you were not there,
Even though I could see your face, your eyes
    Deep within the luminescent screen, elsewhere,
Radiant, streaming out from the sun,
    Sailing, to quote myself, on solar wind.
The other image of you in my mind today
    Is formed of fancy and a blend
Of place names, weather reports, and long novels
    That take place in other places
(Usually by British authors, theologians and scholars
    With disheveled hair and longish faces).
To begin with, the air here is bright and clear
    (A perfect day, for that matter, to walk the dog),
But I hear on the TV news report that Bluefield
    Should expect freezing rain or snow, fog
That will not lift all day. No surprise then
    That I should see you there
In a Bluefield of the mind, a place that's always
    Colder than it is here or anywhere
Nearby, a place that's split in broken mountains,
    That glows an eldritch icy blue
Even though I know that it does not (I have visited
    Or, at least, driven through),
But just now I picture you, walking (or maybe drifting)
    Across a wide and snowy field

(A blue field I would have said but for the pun),
　　　Pressing through icy twigs and branches that do not yield
Until you say the proper words in the proper way.
　　　You are wearing your red corduroy jacket
(The one I complimented) and your golden leggings,
　　　Following an echo, knowing you can track it
Through the cold confusion to its distant source.
　　　Do you see my problem, then?
How do I write a letter to such a person—
　　　An artist lost in space and solar wind
In real time and, at once, that mythic explorer
　　　Lost in rimed Bluefield and the swirling time
Of my imagination? Small wonder that I seldom write
　　　Letters, my personal sin or crime,
The one that one day will do me in and leave me all alone,
　　　Finally abandoned by all my friends,
Left to an empty house, an empty room, an empty mailbox,
　　　Empty head, too, probably, all my just ends.
But I won't brood about my deserts, fair or unfair,
　　　Just now. After all, I *am* writing to you,
Or both of you, and by now I should be used to double vision.
　　　Think of that photo in which I'm split in two,
The one in the coffee-table book: Julia is telling
　　　Us the tale, has everyone's attention
But yours (you're staring off as if to the sun
　　　Or nearby planets), but I guess I should mention
That you're actually thinking of how you'll extend
　　　The story when the turn is yours (you're next),
And I'm there, too, chin in hand, looking right at her
　　　As she spins the tale, relaxed, unvexed,
At ease, but in the mirror there I am, too,
　　　Looking right at you. In time present,
Listening to Julia tell the story; in time future,
　　　In the mirror, caught in the pleasant
Occupation of watching you create the story
　　　Yet to come. It would take Einstein
Or at least Alice through her looking-glass to work out
　　　The equations for your time, mine,

Even Julia's in that scene—all together, all apart,
        All over the place, time bent and refracted,
Scattered and bowed like light through a prism,
        Compressed, intense, let loose, protracted.
And isn't that the way the moment always seems—
        Singular, bifurcated, trifurcate, multiform?
Or, for that matter, the way it has always seemed:
        Whether Heraclitus insisting that the norm
Is always abnormal, the only lasting thing
        That nothing ever lasts, or the astrologer
(Say, Ptolemy or even Paracelsus) who saw
        The planets as a kind of celestial college or
Gathering of the wise, guiding our days
        And nights, in concord or having fights
Among themselves (like any college faculty)
        With the students (us) forced to pay the price.
And what makes it worse, depending on the moment
        Of our first cries in this world,
The lessons are different for us, each and each,
        Relativity displayed, revealed, unfurled:
Uranus ignites Mars, or Mars contacts the Sun,
        Saturn is in retrograde,
Beware of heavy machinery, or, be bold;
        All decisions must be weighed
Against the celestial sway and shove
        Of the planets' every even move.
I know your friend the learn'd astronomer
        Would disapprove
Of my mentioning the truths of the astrologers,
        But even he must admit they taught
And teach us the rules of change, the rule
        Of instability, the flux that ought
To set us free to move but is too often
        The thing we fear (you and I) the most,
That freezes us to the spot, that makes us stoics
        Daring nothing, our only boast
That we cannot lose that which we do not have.
        (But, then, of course, we've lost

Everything before we ever had it, and that
    Seems a dreadful cost
To pay for such minor peace of mind.)
    So, Anita, this is my best attempt
To write a letter to a double-visioned you;
    Chaotic, in order, in control, unkempt,
It is rather like our conversations.
    The day is passing. The cold blue sky,
Clear as a field of ice, is burning to a fiery point
    Of red and gold. I've got to try
To bring things in this letter to a point as well.
    (But when does a poem really ever
Have a point other than itself? All day,
    All night in the atmosphere, never
Being other than its complex, duplicitous self.)
    But I did claim that it has to do
With meaning, so I will try my best
    To leave at least a clue
To what it's (or I'm) about. I've been reading
    George Barker, his words, his thought, his
Vision, who says, "The mystery of the world is this:
    That we do not know what is."
Alone we are born (even twins), the truism says,
    And, our secrets with us, alone we die.
But we are never truly alone at our loneliest,
    Feeling the moon's tug in its passage by,
Knowing the sweep of cosmic dust in our veins,
    Swaying to a music we cannot hear,
Exploring a landscape of despair with only the echo
    Of an echo in our ears.
The images that come to mind, perhaps these are
    The substance of this letter,
Any letter, even those Walt Whitman found
    In the street from God, the weather
Of God's mind on every page, the "kosmos" itself.
    When you try to identify just who you are,
Always remember that the answer is never simple,
    That it depends on the placement of the viewer,

That a photo of the universe from just the right angle
      Might well reveal your features in the stars
And in the empty spaces in between, Alpha Centauri,
      Sirius, the Crab Nebula, Venus, Mars,
A tree of galaxies flowing from your hair,
      The red and gold explosion of the sun
Warming the icy cold of empty space with solar wind.
      And one more thing before I'm done:
It is true we lose the things we hold dearest
      But equally true that because we hold them dear
We find ourselves which we otherwise had lost,
      Find ourselves whole—just now, just here.

SPRING LETTER TO PARADISE

It is, mother, Groundhog Day today,
      Scarcely the first day of spring,
But spring has been in the steep play
      Of light across varied weather,
In the way the birds flit and glide
      By the window, the way the cat
Crouches, switches her tail, begins to slide
      Across the floor to the open door,
A bright day portending six more weeks
      Of bleak winter, just as it did
Last year, a day that always speaks
      Some sort of truth to those
Who listen well. No more winter
      For you then, weeks for us,
For though I found you at the center
      Of life's great mystery,
Still in bed, tucked in, quiet, cold
      As the winter we had yet to live,
You were gone, ninety-one years old,
      "Passed," as Lelani put it,

And what was the last small thing I said
        The night before, "Good night"
Or "Good-bye," before you were dead
        And passed away, gone over, gone?
No matter now. We always liked
        Groundhog Day, its air of prophecy,
Until the actual passage of hours spiked
        Its mystery and turned it into time.
A good day to go, then, all things finally
        Resolved, everything we doubt and fear
And hope made clear, all questions kindlily
        Answered, no secrets, face to face.
If I were to speculate about Paradise, I know
        I'd get it completely wrong,
But I hope there's a place to go
        Or be where with any luck
You can catch Miles and Monk playing
        Together in perfect harmony,
The quartertones all there, saying
        It's all right to Charles Ives
In the audience, who nods his approval.
        And maybe that is the truth
Or at least truth on the slant, one removal
        Or two from something totally different,
Totally the same. But here it isn't spring
        Though spring is on the way, the hyacinths
I planted after your funeral beginning
        Already to appear, green tips
Above the grass, yet still and cold
        In the frigid air today, waiting
For the next warm day, hopeful, bold,
        Neither doubt nor fear bred in the bulb,
As sure of resurrection as Apollo was
        When he planted them in the Greek myth.
A doubled day, then, not far from Christmas,
        Not too much farther to Easter,
Both winter and spring, twinned
        As you sometimes thought I was in your last years,

The nice little boy playing with clothespins,
    Making roadways under the table,
And the graying man with broken eyes,
    A grin as crooked as your arthritic hands,
Saying, "No, there's only me, hard as I try,"
    A whisper of white in a banyan tree
Reflected and lost for a time in our conversation.
    And aren't we all more than we seem,
A community of selves in complex relation,
    All with the same name, often estranged?
Anita is just now claiming that she is six
    Different people at least, and I
Lost count some time ago of my own odd mix
    Of selves imagined, selves constructed,
Selves injured and healed, lost and found again.
    To have them all one, freed of the rule
Of stars and planets, of death and sin,
    Of time and loss and shame, that must
Be Paradise, no matter how we dream it here.
    No, it is not spring, the tree branches
Knotted like old bones, the new buds near
    But still sealed in the dogwood
You planted with your own hands, the one
    I'll have to sell soon along with the house
Where you lived for over forty years, the sun
    Luring the cat to the window,
But not warming the day. The house is silent,
    Anita and Julia are far away. Only time
Is moving in this quiet beauty, violent
    And destructive, wearing away everything
We care for, emptying us into a lonely grave.
    And yet . . . in your voice . . . light
Sings along the glass: *what we truly wish to save*
    We must give away; what we truly wish to keep
We must surrender; what we love will be ours
    Forever. "There is that in me,"
This is Walt Whitman (on my mind today for hours),
    "I do not know what it is—

But I know it is in me." And I know, too,
     How it moves along the soul like light
Along the window pane, leads me to go to
     Seek the day, to find the open door
To Paradise just here, to know to
     Answer the promptings of the heart,
Know for the first time what we all really owe to
     Each other, the debt each day repays.

LISTENING TO THE EDGES

Listening to Bryan Ferry on the car radio,
The thought comes to me like a fist
Or a stone flung back by a passing truck
That I am too grown up not to reason,
Too young not to dream. . . .

This dream slips into mystery,
Into the last secret of eternity:
The heart does not age even as it
Stiffens with plaque, squeezes without rhythm,
Echoes with radio love. . . .

How reasonable, then, to conclude
It is the final trick of the Cosmic Joker,
Eye that cannot see, blind
Gaze that can only find the past
In the mirror's dark glance. . . .

A memory circles like a sharp-shinned hawk,
My mother at ninety shaking her head
With disbelief at the face in her hands,
Yet flirting with the newspaper photographer,
Heart ready to go. . . .

Photography is the mirror I
Cannot deny, succession, the years

Digging in like besieged revetments,
Every past smile a dagger by the eye,
All those loves, all those shadows. . . .

The greatest love, o my love, is
The one we may not have, slipped
In time, ill-timed, out of time,
The sad voice on the car radio
That does not touch the ground. . . .

The greatest love, o my love, is
The one beyond us, the love
That cannot be spoken, that we
Have always hung out to dry
Like Jesus on a twisted tree. . . .

But the dream sustains us
Like the dream you once interrupted,
Your voice clear as a radio song,
To say the one sentence I could not dream,
The secret heart heard. . . .

We cannot escape the love that frees us
In this broken world, our hands
Like claws, our hearts like singing birds,
The trees blossoming like love
In spring, my love, in spring. . . .

BRENDAN GALVIN

PONDYCHERRY

The way some people sing for themselves
on the drive home, I kept repeating
pondycherry out loud, one of those
trivial chunks that pops up,
tangled with the mind's sargassum,

and wondering where I got it, arrived at
a satiny red-brown wood that came
naturally hollowed from the mill, something
a craftsman might use in his furniture,

an elderly woodturner and caner of chairs
who worked out of a storefront, its floor
lovely to the nostrils and eyes
with sawdust and woodcurl.

He'd be a local repository who still used
honeywicket for flicker, *timberdoodle*
for woodcock. He'd look at
a yard-sale chair, its seat busted
through like a basketball hoop, and say,

"That wood's pondycherry, used to be
a stand of it the far side of Higgins Pond.
A pleasure to work with, but the fruit
would pucker you permanent."

Pondicherry, the dictionary gives me,
a former province of French India.
But why should I choose between denotation
and the mind at play, or reject another
hint from the depths under a word
that I've lived other places, other lives?

Skylights

Every October, after a day when something
exotic has landed at the feeder
and waits gasping there as on a prow
far out at sea, a myrtle or Canada warbler
just too wing-beaten to go on,
I wake late to a good dinner
building its cloud above my heart,
and look up where stars in the skylight
on that night alone have a connect-the-dots
logic, a plan I might follow that's pressing
like a template in my head. Then I envision
the great streaming freeways of the birds,
those swerves and swoopings in every
color of feather, three miles up, blurred
crayola streaks a hemisphere long, and
Surinam, French Guiana, Venezuela
loom in a summer down there
like the eminence of a new green heart.
I play around with gravity and magnetic
lines of force trined with the pull of the moon,
but panic hearing the surf of a different
coast in each ear, and drop to name
real hills instead: Tom's and Cathedral
enfolding an arm of river between
bay and ocean; Round and Corn, between
the freshwater lens my pump taps into
and those stars. Husband, father to sleepers,
doorman to dogs, I can't convert pasta
to vector energy anyway. I might say
something I ate causes this,
and tip an invisible nightcap
to the birds, who know where they're going
and how to get there.

For a Daughter Gone Away

Today there've been moments
the earth falters and almost
goes off in those trails of smoke
that resolve to flocks so far
and small they elude my naming.
Walking the old Boston & Maine
roadbed, September, I understand
why it takes fourteen
cormorants to hold the bay's
rocks down. Have I told you
anything you ought to know?
In time you'll come to learn
that all clichés are true, that
a son's a son till he marries,
and a daughter's a daughter
all her life, but today
I want to begin Latin I with you
again, or the multiplication
tables. For that first phrase of
unwavering soprano that came
once from your room, I'd suffer
a year of heavy metal. Let all
who believe they're ready for
today call this sentimentality,
but I want the indelible
print of a small hand
on the knees of my Chinos again,
now that my head's full of
these cinders and clinkers
that refused fire's refinements.
I wish I could split myself
to deepen and hold on as
these crossties have, and admit
goatsbeard and chicory,
bluecurls and blazing star,
these weeds of your never quite

coming back. I wish I could stop
whatever's driving those flocks
and drove the B & M freights into air.

SOME ENTERTAINMENTS SENT WITH A GIFT SNUFFBOX CARVED FROM AN ALLIGATOR'S TOOTH, 1703

I pray this will open prime conversations
for you, and unlock certain minds
across the water. For the alligator
truly is the length of two or three men
from its head, domed like the elephant's,
to the tail, which is flattened
rudderly and as long again
as the body it depends from, and motile
four days when severed. In water
this torso appears first as clusters
of mud, as though the beast were
born of it. But on land it is
mounted on legs like the great tortoise's,
and is horse-thick yet limber and barbed
as a two-man saw. Plated from nape
to tail-tip, it appears hacked
from the stuff of infernal regions.
My first alligator I dragged out of
a fish hawk's grasp when it was
no longer than my foot,
and trained it up on crabs and herring,
until what I hesitate to call gratitude
appeared and strengthened in its nature
at last, and I could with patience
inure it to reins and a light saddle.
After many preliminaries, I galloped
my alligator about the yard

by throwing fishes before it, overlooking
those jaws long as my arms,
which belch blood when it ramps among
its victuals, though I soon
knew that method would not carry me far.
One morning I glimpsed a better way,
and cast out a living goose tied
to a sapling. We were off down
the Jericho road. Horses dumped
their riders and plunged into brush
to avoid that hysterical fowl
fleeing my land sharkfish, which
the Woccons named Toothed-for-Woe.
Me they called *Monwittetan-Wintsohore,*
Alligator Man, for the way my dragon,
inflating itself, squalled so it leveled
a town of the frowardest savages,
pitching their dogs like bowls on a green.
Later I rode it down the Long River
to the shores of that farther ocean,
where it led me to the cask of some
sea robbers, guarded by headless crows,
and showed me the tree-walled meadow
where I heard the woolly mammoth
bellow and stamp, and witnessed its
sweep of tusk and a strangle of
loosestrife in its great trunk.
Such tales as these I might have indited
nolens volens for the greenhorns of London,
who call the beaver a woodchuck, the woodchuck
a muskrat, adventures to fatten myself
and the plagiarists with while I sat
at my fire thirty years, apiss in tea.
But why the upwelling of pity when I see
one of these slough dogs floating becalmed
or rearing its loaf of a head
and lamenting so hotly that steam issues?

Because those eyeslits and terrible
joineries evince unpurgeable sorrow—
as though it remembered its connivance
and was yet flattened beneath the foot of God?

MY FROST DREAM

Farm boys on a hillside in New Hampshire,
shirtsleeves rolled past their elbows,
waiting for a train to pull into a station
down below—Franconia, maybe, or Potter Place—and
take them off to war. A blonde girl stands
by one of them; to get her blue-flowered
'40s housedress and wild beauty on the page,
Frost the botanist compares her
to a roadside weed, the Venus's Looking-glass.
She speaks of merging her father's farm
with her soldier boy's, the dynasty they'll start
after the war. Behind her words Frost's hinting
that the boy won't be coming home, though all
he'll say outright is, "Two farms are more
than twice the work." This poem's more 20th
century than anything of his yet in print,
I tell him, studying the typescript, and since
this is my dream, not Lawrance Thompson's,
he takes the compliment agreeably, and asks
my name. Where are we, Bread Loaf? Cambridge?
We're standing on a sofa making small talk,
our heads way above the party racket. When
X the poet comes by, a voice out of the air
says, "Prepare to be cut dead," and Frost
says, "X, meet Brendan Galvin . . ."

The Portuguese Uncle

There was a grove next door
where we scuffed pine needles
to floor plans for other houses
with no wars over groceries, no
maiden aunts penumbral
with desertion, and no grown-ups
whose remarks to us
nearly disguised their alternate
meanings. Otherwise, we sat
failing on the kitchen steps,
or smoked a hardball through
the morning glories
until Uncle Manny herded us
to his beetle-backed Studebaker
and we drove into his country,
its high smell of fish
snapping us out of it. In rooms
above the wharves talk exploded
in both languages, the one for
cursing hard paymasters
in front of children, the other
for saying the cod went north
and weren't coming back, things
illustrated by hands scored
with the drag of halibut
on droplines. We nursed orange
or grape drinks at enameled
tables, the men sun-browned in
red shirts, with matadors'
smooth hair and noses you tried
not to look at, hands folded
for bottomless silences, in which
to count gulls kiting past
the windows. Once our uncle
yelled "Popeye!" and there he was,
the anchor cap, the squint,

his corncob in that loaf of chin—
at the door of the plant where
women ripped out orange spawn
and dropped it to the floor,
where trawlers sidling to the wharf
shook the world's tin roof
and spiles and at the scales
lumpers and crews might erupt
out of nothing over prices, where
noon-shriek drove those women
arching in their clothes
one by one to the rainbowed water
we'd dare to enter ourselves, sometime,
we said later, alone, and splash
and kick and swim among them
when they came up, lipstick redder,
hair pasted black, wet
to their true shapes.

CAPTAIN TEABAG AND
THE WELLFLEET WITCHES

Red-gold her hair the one night,
a crow's gloss the next, and the tall
or short of her apparently as
she chooses, Silkpocket's the one
who taught me her way of dreaming
where the oysters gather, nights
she'd leave me to my bed alone.
Put it in my head, you might say,
so if I sailed to the dream place
next day I'd drag up such a weight
as would draw the portside
like a lip to the waves. Taught me
a rhyme for summoning breezes
from nowhere even in blue calms,

another for settling tall seas.
Two feats I'd not perform for even
a crowd of one, as per her warning.
Or only once I did, and here's that story:
Off Jeremy one noon it kicked up
some ferocious. My sheets bellied
and it blew a hat-swiper
so the boy hunched to the tiller
two-handed while I crept along
the freeboard like an ape escaping
down a clothesline on all fours,
then crouched in the bow yelling
Silkpocket's verses at the teeth of it,
wind spitting them back drenched,
salting them line by line and driving
every word into my throat and eyes
until I heard because I couldn't see
the canvas crack and flap to
a standstill. Those airs left
whistling in a ball across the headland
and the sun stood out again,
dulling the depths while I dreaded
how I'd catch it from her that night,
for the boy was studying me like
he'd caught me weighting oyster sacks
with stones. Silkpocket taught me . . .
many things. And sure enough, she got
her hooks in me that night out by the Gut,
crooning *Come to me, my palomino.*
Off we went, down the Neck road
at a gallop. You see how my knees
are skunned up yet, for it took us
a few rods before she got me
in the air, my ears between her
cunning thumbs and forefingers
the way you'd turn a key in a lock.
We cleared Shirttail Point
and *Haul those elbows in!* she screeched,

and veered me starboard of that
windmill whicketing around
next the saltworks, then shot us out
up Duck Creek and twice around
the Congregational steeple,
Silkpocket digging those red shoes
in my slats and pushing me at speeds
I lack the sheer for, so by then
I'm chafed and rasped all over.
"We'll have a little drinkie," she says
close to my ear, that mean kind
of babytalk she has, and dips us
in this fog that's dripping over
the Herring River. About that time
I know I'm going to come to alone
and feeling like six sacks of owl pellets
freshmade. Escape her? Sure.
I got as far as Loagy Bay once,
then up come this cloud over the boat
kept changing colors like some gypsy stone
only all its moods was bad? Each way
I tacked it stuck. Calm, flat and blue
was everywhere but where I was.
Then three crows hung up there yacking
under it and the bay commenced to flap
and boil and pitch around, black and oily
as they were. Soon after twenty more
showed up from nowheres, batting around
in the sheets, perched on the gunnels,
tiller, anywhere in the way and everywhere
at once. My gear was a holy tangle
and me with a gaff and as much sense
as a bear in a bee storm slashing around.
All the witches of Wellfleet were there—
Old Margery Gigg the icehouse lady
rode my yawing tiller like a laughing
weathercock. I swung at one and it was
Hamm the postman, I'd know the wrecked

picket-fence of his teeth anywhere,
though up to then I only suspected
he snuck the village's letters home
for something to read, that lonely place
he lives, sunk to the sills in weeds.
Spanish Mariah from out Bound Brook way,
Annie down the oyster shacks,
they were there, and several beansupper
Christians including that moist-handed
Banker Leverett in his sister's bonnet,
gone all to nose and snapping like
a hairless raccoon. Some others
Silkpocket must of sent out of town for,
or signed up in the graveyard. No words I have
could tell you what sobfellows and nobaths
were there, what skroaks and wowsy-eyed
giglets, drabboons, a loptongue or two,
craven-haired skewbabes and bouncies,
pisscutters, bloats, fluffchicks,
retching simps, flarks, bigbighairs
and reeking bone-rigged doglets,
barffleas. Does that add up to
more than twenty? Well I was counting
poorly at the time, and snaggling
about with them in my gear whilst they were
subdividing, tripling, swapping off
one another's best parts all the time
we were going down. Next I know
Silkpocket's got me by the topmost hairs
and hauling me out. "Good grip on you,"
I says, and she says back, "My love
is on the dear one." That being me,
I guess, so how could I escape her
after that? Looks like I'm never
going to know if I'll come to in my bed
or curled up on Holbrook Avenue
one sunrise to the next.

At Ellen Doyle's Brook

Since there's no childhood
without a witch, the children had
some mockery they chanted
in your brogue when they danced
up the dust around your cottage.

Counterpoint to Baileyville's
laundry ghosting on your lines,
was it worse than the silences
their elders used, or is all that
a question of temperament?

As soon pin you down now as capture
your washwater in this stream
they gave your name. You were
different, elusive as your brook's
obscure beginnings and ends,

and sentenced between silences,
you starched their tatted
handkerchiefs you thought were
doilies, amusing to some
even now their song's escaped them.

This water you made yours
a bucket at a time
beats any stone memorial, as the wrecked
millrace attests, and anyone who reads
your moods in leaf-defended

pools—where something gray
whispers itself up to the risk
of one quick sip, or a fleeting yellow
jumps in, spontaneous as a laugh,
and shaking, springs off through the trees—

must see this water underwritten
by hill snows, digesting ice, muscling up
with rain to wash the road out
and beat back underground any prize rose
a lady bequeaths her name.

PELICAN

That look of a singular relic
blown out of the annals
of evolution, such mock-seriousness
turned loose on this world
they might have dubbed me
"Pelican" as early as high school,

not merely for my addiction
to wharves and my vertigo
out of sight of tidal habitats,
but for broad-flippered feet
that still make me
hard to follow on dancefloors,

and for the way, late at night,
trying to make it home
in my black Filene's Basement
clerical trenchcoat (but lined in
cardinal red!), I'd flap
a few strokes, then sail and
flap a few more, the whole getup
assembled to suggest
a saving naïveté.

Then there's my approach to
necessity, not the direct sharp
plunge of a gannet, all torque

to an economical vanish, but
the splash of some bulk
a deckhand rolls over the side
as soon as land
has cleared the horizon.

If they stuck around
after that splatter, they'd have
seen it was all in knowing
the exact angle for entry,
sheer technique so I come up
sitting every time, making
those swallowing movements
that assure I will never
go hungry, operating on
too many levels at once,
the usual crowd of laughing gulls
hanging around for crumbs.

CORNCRAKE

To take the rust off the needle
in its haystack, try this:
Isle of Lewis, Outer Hebrides,
a grownover field on its north tip,
and a corncrake sounding somewhere in
knee-high grass like your thumb
run down the tines of a comb.
Elusive field-soul, quail-size
and feathered like the field, heard
less and less since tractors began
against the eggs' stillness.
Wade in and risk being taken for
a retired farmer, his plowhorse
sold, walking a straight furrow
as if hitched in the traces of dementia,

left to right and reversing all the way
into the depth of field, while this
voice thrower's there, now over
there, until the cliffs begin
and a few feet away kittiwakes turn
above ocean boiling on stone.
And the corncrake? Silent. Or gone,
though you've still never seen it fly.
The one right word in the whole
thesaurus of field may have crouched
between your feet as you passed
troubling the grass over it.

Saint Brendan's Psalm

from *Saints in Their Ox-Hide Boat*

Doctor of our hearts, now we are as
murderers cast adrift, and would
gladly change vessels with sailors
on some glassy tide, who see
beneath them the boar-headed,
swallow-tailed ones turning bellies
pale as the drowned toward them,
and ones like swollen chestnut husks
and pincered, and other ribbony ones,
many-legged, tusked, lugworms
a weakening mind magnifies. For now
You raise a black wind from the north,
or send against us a gray west wind,
and we long for the barking of a fox
from a field's threshold after
first nocturn. Openmouthed on the edge
of every wave, we are lifted toward heaven.
Then—as our bellies drink our souls
like liquid fire—dropped

to a narrow glen. The light is
in turmoil, and our wits are useless
as cups of thrown water. We stagger this
way and that, take hold like men
by drink taken hold of and cry out
in our trouble, and hope down into the oak,
which groans for its roots again.
Each stringer of ash, bound ankle and wrist
in thongs, is a captive without reprieve,
crying out for the north side of
the mountain and a thrush at its berries.
The tree our saws drew the least
scantling from was seeded by Your hand,
and the oak's heart in our rails.
Even the ox hides we tanned in pits
of oak bark and stitched
with threads of flax, and wool grease
we slathered on our sheep-smelling hull
to keep the sea out. Therefore
our boat is from Your hand, *is*
Your right hand under us when we forsake
every heart-softening face—our white
martyrdom—for the emptiness of this
seal pasture where every angel-haunted
abbey stone sinks out of memory
and the salt blears consolations of
heather and harebell, things grown
large in our eyes. Clench Your fingers
in each stitch of flax as You did
in the roots when the weed flowered
blue against darker, wind-worked loughs,
for our mast whips sky, and our sail
is a fleeing rag. As You put breath
in the ox, breathe now with our
sea-trampler flexing its ribs to fit
water, Your eyes quick for the first
drips from faults the warblefly made
when this beast-boat plowed our fishless
fields, for we sail from bowl to bowl,

BRENDAN GALVIN

dragging the world with us, uphill
in all directions while our souls
touch bottom, longing for meadow-quiet
and a sea reflecting stars, not this
wave-beheading wind wherein the steersman
dares not look astern, but hangs like
a bug on a straw, and petrels creep
up the sides of the water.

NIMBLEJACKS

Remember Hot Spats and the Kaiser,
who illustrated the beautiful
moving-while-standing-still word
"nimblejack," a word worthy of
a class of sailboats, like sneakbox,
or sharpie? I'm talking soupbeards
and rent-laggards like Boofer,
who checked out the coinbox on every
pay phone in town. I'm talking
skew-footed Dr. Highpockets, who'd share
the sandwich in his carrot bag with anyone.
When was the last time Pungie
yawped at you across the street to say
how well that new puddle was doing
on the wrong side of the dike?
How about Tick, and the Man of Steel,
walk-ons from normality's hinterland,
part of the 9% who never have an opinion?
They were the canaries in our mine shaft,
our early warning systems, and never
disappeared into the shops all day,
but stayed on the sidewalks to hinder
the broom of the future simply by being there.
Not one ever asked, "Are you affiliated
with any academic institution?"
or propped Einstein's essays

strategically in a window of the Land Rover,
but remember how they used to line us up
in their sights on Main Street,
leaning left and right to keep us level?

Getting Through

a little disquisition for my daughter

In one of my dreams somebody
in a white apron's always
yelling "Come back, you beatnik,"
as I slam out of there just
in time. Water too hot
for human hands is glissading
over the lip of a sink,
or a manager in a paper hat
is threatening, "You don't want
to leave here with a bad taste
in your mouth." Always
the place is hanging over
a mudslide, the river out back
is rising toward warped 2 × 4s
and I've just said the magic words.
Let the bosses wrestle the sparking
wire or the customer who has to say
the horsemeat's for his dog
every time. How pure a moment
that first one on the pavement.
Even in dreams I breathe original air.
There's a car full of girls and beer
and we're off to the Cape
in a May dusk. That's the ticket
all right, but the ride has to lead
to the place called Sunday evening,

where the fun implodes like
a morning glory: work is the father
of gravity, so whatever went up
comes back down on the ground
in sensible shoes. Cerebral pickpockets
who hustle The Dignity of Labor
never busted a table or tossed
a caesar salad under the noses
of shrinks on vacation, as you have,
and too much of our time on the planet
is spent discovering things
we don't want to do for too long.
Nevertheless, we arrive by subtraction,
the way a sculptor knocks stone away
until Crazy Horse and his pony
lean into the pure breeze of intention.

SNAKEBIT, 1752

Six foot of mingled orange, tawny,
and black, its underside leaden,
a rattlesnake I kept for study
in an empty rum keg, thinking the vapors
would befuddle him, one morning
lay in wait under that cover when I came
with a snared chipmunk, and struck
my hand, pumping green poison in.

I knew I had only minutes, so cornered
a chicken in the yard, breaking her neck
with a quick upward jerk, and with
the selfsame knife as I had hacked
my murderer to portions, which yet rolled
and snapped along the floor as though
each worked to produce its own head,
I split the hen's belly and plunged

the insulted hand into her still-working
jellies and hot lights, whereon I swear
the thing's feathers wilted and began
dropping away.

     That serpent I kicked
piece by piece to the hearthfire, and soon
began a splutter and popping of fats,
a whooshing of steam among the flames,
while on my hand the fowl, now black
as though itself roasted there,
stunk in a way the Devil was in the room.
It too I added to the fire, its vile smoke
offered heavenward, then wrapped the hand
with a plaster.

     Along their routes
veins stood and flared to the elbow,
though I plunged the arm in a bucket of
vinegar and waited upon Fate. A tree
tingled and grew from the tips of my
fingers, swelling itself up my forearm
until with a razor I opened my palm
and let my own blood flow.

I rolled and steeped some days upon my bed,
waking at times to discover the arm itself
a mottled snake, its arrowhead buried
and drinking at the chambers of my heart.
In dreams and awake I was rolled in lowly places,
sumps of the deepest hollows, among the pulp
and lichens of tumbled, ancient deadfall,
cobwebbed, prickled with my own drenched bedding.

At times I even seemed to myself a tree,
toes feeling downward toward groundwater,
at my extremities these woody prongs,

scaled, soft-pithed, where juices
wended toward the terminal buds,
which were lapped over and sometimes
in my fevers flowered, blue-lipped,
orange at heart, or rosy and black-veined,
and again like gold-wormed feather dusters.

I was possessed at times with fears and watchings.
Then vermin drew near, their faces large
as my own, lights malefic in their ebony eyes,
each sentient hair distinct, their mouth parts working,
warning against ambulations into their kingdoms.

Some evenings I was settled with cooler moments,
and at dusk, from the swamp and beyond,
a surf of sound arose as from another village
in there. I could pick out some drunkard or
madwoman's denials, but not attach them
to the screech owl, and sounds like someone
hacking brush, and breaths blown across
the mouths of flasks.

               I reflected how these
mortal troubles began when I listened almost
from the cradle while the yellow rail sounded,
and a flycatcher whistled, desultory. Later
I stood hours on the threshold of that
bush world, thinking the pygmy owl's bark
a pup crying somewhere, boxing the air
at the end of its tether, and one day
entered a few feet in.

               Now at times it seemed
I wandered unattended in landscapes where maroon
leaves of the oak formed metallic masks,
and was observed from thickets by eyes cognizant
of my passage there, and heard such chuckles,
small laughter and rattling, I imagined the mice
dicing, hands pressed on their mouths.

In the few hours of clarity vouchsafed me,
I was capable of depicting the seed vessel of
a lotus, with threatening holes
where the pips were cast, and land snails
nearby, and a rubythroat in arrested flight,
grasping a serpentine branch above
a hollowed log whose sockets menaced me.

That bird stares where a green lizard
emerges from a cover of pickerelweed,
engorging a bullfrog by the head, the frog's
feet clawing air. A green miasma ran in me yet.

Under My Stornoway Hat

Thinking along its designs
that look like the mingled sea routes
of wandering Picts, Celts,
and Norsemen, mumbling the names
of their ports, I see how Scalloway
might render to scallawag,

how all my life, hanging around
harbors, three sheets to the wind
on their air of departures alone—
roadstead, outward bound,
hull down for anywhere, a lingo
that lifts my nape hairs—

I might have become a seaport's
drunk if poems hadn't
grabbed me by the throat.
If I say Caledonian-MacBrayne,
my pulse rate drops and I'm ready
to sail on just my name

for Stromness or Lerwick or Ullapool,
anywhere oystercatchers and lapwings
stand in for lowly pigeons,
places precipitated onto the sea-line
because they're too blue
for the sky, lumps of holy island
blue as the wool of this hat,
that now and again disappear

and return with more curlews
in a single field than I've counted
in a lifetime. Here in this livingroom,
in this magical blue hat, I see
how Stornoway commends itself
to stowaways, and this sheep-smelling
wool recalls the Soay ram
who told me, side-of-his-mouth
near Scrabster, Keep moving.

THE MAIDEN UNCLES

Around and around the inner
wall of a barrel
three stories deep he rode
an Indian motorcycle
so oily it looked explosive,
and the miracle over,
dismounted and walked away
through touchable awe
into a carnival crowd of
forty years ago, wearing
the same singed-rabbit
expression he'd begun with,
as if to say, "So what?
I defy gravity several times
nightly, and I win."

It's his eyes locked in
neutral that recall
the maiden uncles to me now.
In households up and down
the block there was a Jocko,
John, Jacko, or plain Jack,
as though all the variations
translated to bachelor, living
quietly on the sufferance of
a married sister, like dowry
or the family's shadow embodied.

They were stand-in cooks
and baby sitters, unbidden
mowers of lawns, essentially
silent, without mystery,
neither gassed on the Somme
nor left at the altar, as needless
of money or a thing
it could provide as those
comic strip characters who reflect
the room's windows on their eyes.

Too early for aliens
to have withdrawn some organ
crucial to action, but were they
changelings, their real selves
displayed on Harleys or wearing
bulletproof vests in some
swap shop down the galaxy?

No brother-in-law ever yelled,
"Dammit, Jack, that's a million
dollar idea!" or "Get the hell out!"
And you'd think some fact
of their common experience
might have drawn them into
fraternity, a storefront lodge

with Order of Youngest Siblings
on the window, at least a bar
on a corner, but they never
actually seemed to see
each other, just waited out
whatever it was, no rage,
no ecstasy, reminders
how vice and risk distinguish
the rest of us to each other.
Ours, preparing the pot
of an afternoon,
would sometimes venture
without a shadow of complaint,
"We're always
the last to have our tea."

An American Naturalist Writes to a Londoner, 1758

Now I will tell you our manner
of gardening here, which progresses
not by calendar, but by natural signals.
On a clear March night, I sight down
the Dipper's bowl for a backwards
question mark, tail of the rising Lion,
and then may be found slapping mud
from the plot into balls, squeezing
to test for water content, this before
even a single mallard clacks from
the creek, and last year's pumpkins
seem the wreckage of its quarter moons.
Then the whole plot is already staked
in my head, minus slugs, borers,
hornworms, loopers, beetles and all
that plague I forget each year
until they descend like a host of

savages to be bought off
only by a feast of this or that leaf,
and dug out of vines and stems
where they poke without welcome.
Asparagus I intercrop with parsley,
since I have discovered they agree
with one another. The latter germinates
long, and is said to go to the Devil
and back nine times ere it breaks
the soil, but I have found it mild
and without evil influence. Beans
I keep far from onions they can't
abide, and basil, which breeds
a merry heart, I grow along borders
with umbelliferous dill, whose leaves
are agreeable with fish, though of
a strength not to everyone's taste.
These strong-scented herbs, with chives
and mint, may keep a barrier against
insects, though my studies here
need more attention. Native squashes
and gourds are set when the dogwood
flowers, and tomatoes during
the mayfly hatch. This conveys somewhat
our manner of gardening. I would
continue but that in the mere telling
I grow fatigued, and must ask myself why,
yearly, I engage in it with such ardor
since I am without family. For the surety
of plenty, or the images such growth
alone provides, or because I do better
with vegetable kind than human,
no easy admission, and have come to
myself more than once knocking upon
and addressing a blue squash
of five-stone weight and pebbled like
the back of an alligator? By the time
of the Perseids, when my turnips go in

for autumn, I am as weary as some
old king fighting his battle with
the sea, down on hands and knees in that
riptide of beans and cabbage splashes,
a spume of chickweed flying over
my shoulders, wishing I had never listened
for spring peepers chiming their long,
ghostly sleighrides through the dark.

Walter Anderson Sleeping on the Levee

In New Orleans to research Hurricane Betsy,
the one he'd ridden out tied to a tree trunk
on Horn Island, he rolled up for the night
on the levee by Audubon Park, letting
the Mississippi talk him to sleep.
Surrounded again, as on the island,
toward morning he felt the serious eyes,
and waited on the moment they'd show themselves.
He saw for the one and only time
the carcasson, then the smaragdine
and gallowglass, but were these the names
of birds, or the names of birds
he wished there were? If a bird is a hole
in heaven through which a man may pass,
then what in the hell were all these anxious
steppers? No pouldeau or pelican, nothing
he'd ever sketched or done in watercolors,
no redwing or boat-tailed grackle
that waited for raisins and cold rice
he'd fling them from last night's supper.
The hurricane, he figured, had lifted
these strangers out of the park's aviary.
Could they sense that he'd talked with
the morning star, or escaped from hospitals

because authority amused him? He was
necessary again: on the levee these birds
would starve or be brought down by
an air rifle or household beast. Casting
bread crumbs over his shoulder, he led them
back into the park, wrestling their names
from himself, pied piper of the stonechuck
and pripet, the fireneck, peabill,
mer-hen, the garget, the stant.

Letter Accompanying the Specimen of an Amazing Bird, 1763

If shipboard rats
haven't worried this little beauty
out of condition entirely,
and it has escaped those meddlesome
sorts of sailors who jimmy shipments
with a nose for liquors preserving
specimens, you will see here
a thing which in your old world
has no counterpart. These sleep
all winter, though none among
the Wampanoags can tell me where.
In summer, when I myself so love
to nap in the influence of flowers,
I have been roused by a sudden
buzzy agitation in the bell of
a trumpet vine. At first nothing
is there, then one of these
flower birds, or bird flowers—
they are so ornamented—will fly
backwards out, as quick in
reverse motion as forward,
for they go up, down, sideways
and continuous, and can stand

upon air with only a minor arousal
of it, then brief and direct as
a shooting star proceed to
a grass-pink or trillium to siphon
fragrance through their tubular beaks,
thence perhaps to the lips
of the red turtlehead blossom.
I conclude that they live solely
upon these aromas, favoring
oranges and reds because their vapors
produce the most energy. You will
not be surprised to discover that
I have tried this airy diet myself,
and for days have gone about
without other sustenance, intruding
my nose in blooms, sniffing essences,
careful not to seal the exit of a bee
or whatever else, until my rebellious
appetite drove me to clean out
the cupboard. But would I could drive
the bung home on those fellows
in your country who pronounce upon
our stingy air and unfruitful weathers—
for here's a bird that thrives
upon them! Their own sky is but
a ceiling ringed with painted nymphs,
and could I drop one of those
shrimplings overboard, just as
a great ray is passing, its breadth
that of two gentlemen's cloaks,
it wouldn't fail to elevate
the hairs along his wretched neck.
Or if I could discover the means
of sending across to you a living moose,
its rack like a tree and so plattered
a banquet could be set upon it,
a herd of your deer could cavort
beneath its legs, and posed before it

you would make no more effect than
milady's lapdog. It is true we have
no ruins, no cathedrals, but therefore
no weight of history to wrestle
as a farmer his pasture stones,
only mountains that heave like ocean,
as fit as Sinai for receipt of
prophecy, sublime for the unfolding
of immortality, and waters upon
the landscape equal to a clear eye
in an honest face, and trees which,
were they men, would be grand
originals, models for busts
and frescoes worthy of log houses.
The specious politeness of your
enervated world we are without,
and its disguises. Would we cringe
like toads, our backs mimicking
leaves spotted with decay, not to
offend or disturb? Who meets
an American meets him square-toed,
square-faced in open air, nose out,
the prow of his countenance
broached to whatever weather.
But I am straying from my path again.
The scarlet wimple on the throat
of this bird seems black
in weak light. Other times it passes
through changes that emulate
the tinctures of those flowers it
loves best. I have watched
a female collecting milkweed silk
and down of ferns, saddling them
to an underleaf branch with stolen
spider web and the strings of
caterpillars, then implanting
this device with tree moss.
Hence the nest which I enclose,

its cup formed when the industrious
bird works her body down, fitting it
to the central mass, forming the cup
preparatory for these two eggs
or twin white beans, which are merely
seeds, perhaps more secret in
their processes, but led by the same
warmth and moisture to similar
increase of life. Mantises,
dragonflies, frogs, even
the gummy spider web are these humbird's
nemeses, though one of these
flying fractions will drive after
a crow with the persistence of
a winged augur. An early frost, too,
will stun them from the air
before they can make for winter sleep,
whereby I go about among the trees
collecting them like fruit.

A Cold Bell Ringing
in the East

It woke me to this full moon
just pulling away
from the skylight's pine,
and fire in the stove's window
faint as two owls courting
somewhere in these empty woods.
Was it the cold I let in
when I let the dog out
that reduced everything to images,
stripping the rags off ego
and abstraction, shivering
the shadows of the pines?
In this light all our attempts

at this or that mean nothing,
we live by understanding less
than there is in the nose
of this dog construing the air.
That pine is no inn,
the moon's no Chinese courtesan
departing from it a thousand
years ago, and I am not Li Po.
There are those who envy that stone
its decoder-ring luminosity, and those
who would sell the tree.
What joy in having been at all,
in feeding the fire and knowing
that everything isn't about us.
Who can witness these moments
and edges otherwise, except someone
outside them, without
the camouflage of a horned lark,
and praise the virtues of scrub pines
with guardian shapes of sky
among them on these hills?
Only someone not woven into
that fabric, with no protective
coloring, who sees where a deer
is first air, then color of dusk
in scrub, then dusk itself,
with its air of invisible mending.

GEORGE GARRETT

LUCK'S SHINING CHILD

Because I am broke again
I have the soles of my shoes repaired
one at a time.

From now on one will always be
fat and slick with new leather
while his sad twin,

lean and thin as a fallen leaf,
will hug a large hole like a wound.
When it rains

one sock and one foot get wet.
When I cross the gravel parking lot
one foot winces

and I have to hop along on the other.
My students believe I am trying
to prove something.

They think I'm being a symbol of
dichotomy, duality, double-dealing,
yin and yang.

I am hopping because it hurts.
Because there is a hole in my shoe.
Because I feel poor for keeps.

What I am trying not to do
is imagine how it will be in my coffin,
heels down, soles up,

all rouged and grinning above my polished shoes,
one or the other a respectable brother
and one or the other

that wild prodigal whom I love
as much or more than his sleek companion,
luck's shining child.

Abraham's Knife

Where hills are hard and bare,
rocks like thrown dice, heat
and glare that's clean and pitiless,
a shadow dogs my heels, limp
as a drowned man washed ashore.
True sacrifice is secret, none
to applaud the ceremony, nor
witness to be moved to tears.
No one to see. God alone
knows, Whose great eye winks not,
from Whom no secrets are hid.

My father, I have loved you,
love you now, dead so many years.
Your ghost shadows me home.
Your laughter and your anger still
trouble my scarecrow head like wings.
My own children, sons and daughter,
study my stranger's face. Their flesh,
bones frail as a small bird's,
is strange, too, in my hands.
What will become of us?
I read my murder in their eyes.

And you, old father, Abraham,
my judge and executioner, I pray
bear witness for me now. I ask
a measure of your faith. Forgive
us, Jew and Gentile, all
your children, all your victims.

In naked country of no shadow
you raise your hand in shining arc.
And we are fountains of foolish tears
to flood and green the world again.
Strike for my heart. Your blade is light.

REVIVAL

Now chaos has pitched a tent
in my pasture, a circus tent
like a huge toadstool
in the land of giants. Oh,
all night long the voices of
the damned and saved keep me
awake and, *basso,* the evangelist.
Fire and brimstone, thunder and lightning,
telegrams in the unknown tongue!
The bushes are crawling with couples.
I see one girl so leafy that
she might be Daphne herself.

I know there were giants once,
one-eyed wonders of the morning
world. Ponderous, they rode
dinosaurs like Shetland ponies,
timber for toothpicks, boulders for
baseballs, oceans for bathtubs,
whales for goldfish. Great God,
when they shook fists and roared,
stars fell down like snowflakes
under glass! Came then Christ
to climb the thorny beanstalk
and save us one and all.

ARE YOU SAVED ?????
Rocks are painted, trees nailed

with signs, fences trampled.
Under the dome of the tent
falls salt of sweat and tears
enough to kill my grass at the roots.
Morning and I'll wake to find
the whole thing gone. Bright dew
and blessed silence. Nothing
to prove they camped here and tried
to raise a crop of hell except
that scar of dead space (where the tent was)
like a huge footprint.

SOLITAIRE

The days shuffle together.
Cards again? No, no, I mean
like convicts in lockstep,
like the patients on the Senile Ward
I saw once, gray and feeble,
blank-eyed creatures in cheap cotton,
pumped full of tranquilizers
("It's the only efficient way to handle
the situation," an attendant told me),
so lethargic they could hardly pick up their feet.

The gray days shuffle together.
The trees are picked and plucked,
sad tough fowl not fit for stewing.
The round world is shaved and hairless
like the man in the moon. Screams,
but I can't hear it. Next door
the dog howls and I can.
Break out a fresh deck for God's sake!
Bright kings and queens and one-eyed jacks.
Free prisoners. And let the old men go home.

For a Bitter Season

The oak tree in my front yard dies,
whose leaves are sadder than cheap wrapping paper,
and nothing I can do will keep it long.

Last spring in another place a pear tree
glistened in bloom like a graceful drift of snow.
Birds and bees loved that spacious white

and a daughter was born in the time of flowers.

Now I am a stranger and my oak tree dies
young. Blight without a name, a bad omen.
I die, too, fret in my familiar flesh,

and I take this for a bitter season.
We have lived too long with fear. We take
fear for granted like a drunken uncle,

like a cousin not quite all there
who's always there. I have lived too long
with the stranger who haunts my mirror.

Night in the city and the sirens scream
fresh disasters for my morning paper.
The oak tree in the front yard dies.

Bless us, a houseful of loving strangers,
one good woman, two small boys, a man
waking from sleep to cough his name.

And bless my daughter made of snow and bluest eyes.

ITALIAN LESSON

from "Some Snapshots"

When I hear of the death of another major poet these days,
I remember Rome, 1958, myself standing alongside an enormous priest
by a newspaper kiosk in Trastevere, staring at headlines—
IL PAPA E MORTO! As the priest turns away a voice from the crowd
(all too poor to buy a paper) calls out: "Is it true the Holy Father is dead?"
The priest nods, then shrugs hugely and answers in the local dialect:
"Better him than us, eh? Better him than us." And walks off to his chores
among the poor who are always with us even until the end of the world.

CROWS AT PAESTUM

The crows, a hoarse cone in the wind,
a swarm of flies, so small and busy
they seem, so tossed by breeze
from mountains where the snow
glitters like a brooding skullcap,
the crows, I say, swirl and cry out
and rise to be torn apart in tatters,
a shower of burnt cinders, fall
in one swoop to a perch in the sun
on the lee side of a Grecian temple.

Sheep, too. Soft music of light bells.
I have seen them grazing in other ruins,
cropping the shadowed grass
among the broken emblems of empire
and once with the dome of St. Peter's
for background, behind and above them
like a gas balloon on a string.
There behind me posed Garibaldi,
bronze above a squalling traffic circle.
Now crows and sheep and a yawning guard

share the ruins of the Paestum with me.
The wind off the mountains chills
and westward the sea is white-capped, too,
is all of sparkling like new-minted coins.
"And they came nigh unto the place
and there builded a great city."
To what end? That a Greek relic
should tug the husband and the wife
from snug *pensione* with camera and guidebook?
For a few tinkling sheep and the exploding crows?

I am uneasy among ruins, lacking
the laurel of nostalgia, the romantic wand,
and cannot for a purpose people empty places
with moral phantoms and ghostly celebrations.
I listen to the soft bells. I watch
the crows come to life again,
sheer off and fall to wrestling the wind,
thinking: "If sheep may safely stand
for that which, shorn and dipped,
is naked bleating soul, why then

I take these crows, whose name
is legion, for another of the same:
the dark, the violent, the harsh
lewd singers of the dream, scraps
of the shattered early urn, cries
cast out, lost and recovered, all
the shards of night. Cold air
strums the fretted columns and
these are the anguished notes
whose dissonance is half my harmony."

EGYPTIAN GOLD

The pickpockets of Rome
are clever as any of their kind

I've ever known. They can
lift a wallet from your pocket
with less touch than the breeze.
They can disembowel a pocketbook
while it hangs, idle, on a lady's arm,
and she'll never notice it until,
home with a sigh, she flings
it on the table where it lies
like a cleaned fish. And when
they work in duets and trios,
as for example at the *Stazione Termini,*
it's with the precision of ballet.
They thrive on difficulty.
Button your coat, hold onto your purse
like a new baby, and nevertheless
your property is theirs if they
have a mind to take it.

But private property isn't
our proper topic just now.
I don't own much, it's true;
and it isn't likely that either
pickpockets or poets
will ever be rich enough to care.

The point is:
what happens when you fall among thieves?
And who, Lord, is my neighbor?
Jesus Christ, who knew one thief
from another, had the answer
for a lawyer to ponder on,
a hard saying. There is just one
Samaritan. The rest of us
lie naked and beaten in the ditch.
Now, in an age when thievery
is so refined it calls itself
Success, when to be stripped and beaten
is to be foxed, when all grapes

go to the vineyard keeper,
and nobody, early or late,
draws any wages, and we applaud
the blind man leading the blind,
I feel like saying with P. T. Barnum—
"This Way To The Egress!"

But then I must call to mind
Saint Augustine glossing Exodus,
explaining why God gave permission
for Moses to take along Egyptian gold
and showing how this means
that all things belong to God.
And if we are going to build
new temples we might as well
use the marble of the pagans.
And if we're going to tell the truth,
we'd better gut the pocketbooks
of all the poets who tried and failed.
As we pass by their honored biers,
we'll pick the pennies from their eyes.

I'm pleased by the Roman pickpockets.
As I said, they never get rich,
and finally their fingers lose the art,
stiffen out of subtlety
(just as sweet singers grow hoarse).
And they end up wistful on corners
watching a new generation strut
sassy and unplucked past them.
As long as they don't get my passport,
I'll praise them and their skill.

But I don't want to leave the impression
of an American overseas
and overawed by all that's foreign.
My grandfather lost his good gold watch
in an elevator at the Waldorf.

Buzzard

I've heard that holy madness is a state
not to be trifled with, not to be taken
lightly by jest or vow, by lover's token
or any green wreath for a public place. Flash
in the eyes of madmen precious fountains,
whose flesh is wholly thirst, insatiate.

I see this graceful bird begin to wheel,
glide in God's fingerprint, a whorl
of night, in light a thing burnt black,
unhurried. Somewhere something on its back
has caught his eye. Wide-winged he descends
like angels to the business of this world.

I've heard that saintly hermits, frail, obscene
in rags, slack-fleshed, eyes like jewels, kneel
in dry sand among the tortured mountains, feel
at last the tumult of their prayers take shape,
take wings, assume the brutal rush of grace.
This bird comes then and picks those thin bones clean.

For Tiresias

from "Eight Lyrics"

Speak to us who
are also split.
Speak to the two
we love and hate.

You have been both
and you have known
the double truth
as, chaste, obscene,

you were the lover
and the loved,
you were the giver
who received.

Now tell us how
we can be one
another, too.
Speak to us who

in single wrath
cannot be true
to life or death.
Blinder than you.

OR DEATH AND DECEMBER

The Roman Catholic bells of Princeton, New Jersey,
wake me from rousing dreams into a resounding hangover.
Sweet Jesus, my life is hateful to me.
Seven A.M. and time to walk my dog on a leash.

Ice on the sidewalk and in the gutters,
and the wind comes down this one-way street
like a deuce-and-a-half, a six-by, a semi,
huge with a cold load of growls.

There's not one leaf left to bear witness,
with twitch and scuttle, rattle and rasp,
against the blatant roaring of the wrongway wind.
Only my nose running and my face frozen

into a kind of a grin that has nothing to do
with the ice and the wind or death and December,
but joy pure and simple when my black and tan puppy,
for the first time ever, lifts his hind leg to pee.

Romantic

I've heard some jealous women say
that if your skin were cut away
and tacked upon a public wall,
it would not please the eyes at all.

They say your bones are no great prize,
that hanging in the neutral breeze
your rig of ribs, your trim of thighs
would catch no fetching harmonies

but tinkle like a running mouse
over piano keys. They hold
that, stripped, your shabby soul
will whimper like a vacant house

you are so haunted. "Ask
her," they say, "if she'll unmask.
Let her shed beauty like winter trees.
Time will bring her to her knees."

Still, I must have you as you are,
all of a piece, beautiful and vain,
burning and freezing, near and far,
and all my joy and all my pain.

And if you live to scrub a floor
with prayer, to weep like a small ghost,
which of us will suffer more,
who will be wounded most?

Fat Man

O flesh, my tyrant wife, my shrew,
old slattern, what's to become of you?

Of us? It's true I've come to hate
the way you smirk from mirrors, float
in steaming tubs, sweat on summer days
or, shameless, writhe in nets of eyes
that measure all your bulk and girth.
It's you I love although I curse your birth.

What is to love? To love's to dance.
The spirit leads the flesh. Without a wince
the flesh should follow and should smile.
A map of all of you shows miles
of frowns. I study you and weep
for pity's sake—the only crop I reap.
I'll never leave you, cruel and fair,
who leave me panting halfway up the stair.

Envoy

Little poem, the two of us know too much.
You and I can never be quite the same again.

I pretend I am gray from worrying over you
while you profess to be concerned about my health.

Walking along together, father and frisky daughter,
holding hands, we are ready to greet friends or enemies.

And I grin, thinking to myself: *You little bitch!*
Nobody else can love you and I couldn't care less.

But you know better: *The old man will eat his heart out,*
ravenous for the love and kisses of strangers.

Cracking and fading like an old photograph,
I am pleased to bequeath the same fate to you.

All supple and shiny now, my son,
you picture my skull and bones on a stone.

You know what happens on the dusty playgrounds,
the raw taste of knuckles, the colors of a bruise.

I know about steppes and tundra of blank paper
and stinking jungles where words crawl like snakes.

Both of us hear voices and believe whatever they say.
In dreams we meet monsters and hold them like lovers.

We shall never talk to each other about any of this.
In all due time I hope to forget your proper name.

Grip tight, little one. Hold your head high.
Strut, you bastard, and smile at the people.

An Epigram by Martial

from "Three More Short Ones"

To the reader: when you look
inside, you're bound to find here
some good verses, some middling, and I fear
plenty of bad ones. What can I say?
Buddy, it's the only way
a poet can make a book.

Manifesto

for R. H. W. Dillard

to begin again

after a long time
and many promises
not to say anything
not to add another voice
to the damned cacophony
cacophony of the damned
makers of verses
spinning prayerwheels
of speculation & gossip
fast & faster
till the words are gone
all voices howl & moan
becoming at last
the humming tune
of a whirling top

o prayerwheels & tops
who is able
to translate you

who reads you
loud & clear

avoid poets
as once ancestors
carefully avoided
lepers with little bells

evade eloquence
a beggar's palm
hungry for coins

elude logic
a clenched fist
to break noses

how many times
facing a waste
of blank paper
have I said
nothing no not one
not one least leaf
falling to flame or
flagging the spring's
first & final heat
not one southward
surge of birds
nor even the song
of their returning
not laughter & tears
neither body dreaming
nor mind gambling
nor spirit kneeling. . . .

no swore I   no   nothing
under sun & moon
will make me begin again
who has wrestled angels
feeling flesh wither
who has danced with demons
drunk on all fours
knows what I mean
who for all honor
has yet said
instead of keeping
holy silence
has left unsaid
when words were kisses
knows I mean well

who too much has seen
of naked untruth
too often heard
the old songs pass
like dirty pennies
from palm to palm
he reads me
loud & clear

yet have I today
shameless gone forth

o damned cacophony
what have I done

confess
I bought a notebook
and a new fountain pen

to begin again
ring little bells
to begin

The pen is red.

WONDERFUL PEN: A SNAPSHOT

When I bought this wonderful pen this morning,
at Ulrich's on South University in Ann Arbor,
the lady escorted me personally to the checkout counter,
maybe because I might try to sneak out without paying
but also because it was clearly a kind of an occasion
for me and for her and (I guess) for the store.
After all, how often does someone just walk in here
and ask for and pay cash for a $185 fountain pen?

The lady tells the girl at the cash register
what the pen costs and that I get a faculty discount
of 10%. Casually, then, I peel off and plunk down
four $50-bills, poor old U. S. Grant on the front of each.
It is payday, and I am feeling good, feeling fine.
I have been saving a long time for this stubby black Mont Blanc
with its bright gold nib which is sure to teach me some golden words.
I smile. Girl glares back her altogether savage disapproval.
"Jesus Christ!" she exclaims. "People are starving in places like Bangladesh!
They are killing each other with clubs in Uganda and Cambodia!
And you—I can't fucking *believe* it!—are spending a fortune
on a fountain pen! What can you possibly *do* with a pen like that?"
Saddened, embarrassed, but refusing to feel guilty, what can I say?
"Lady, this pen takes moving pictures; it records human voices and
if you stick it all the way up your ass, you'll find that you can sing
more sweet songs than a canary or a Georgia mockingbird."

Little Movie without a Middle

The big bad abstractions are back in town again.
Tall, slope-bellied, shaded by wide-brimmed hats,
dragging their huge shadows by the heels, they swagger
down the empty street. A hound dog rises from his snooze
near the swinging doors of the Red Eye Saloon and slinks away
without even pausing to stretch, boneless as poured water.
Chink-a-chinka-chink, bright spurs warn the dusty world.
Beneath an enormous sombrero, a Mexican crosses himself,
and then continues to snore more loudly than before.
Acting more on inspiration than logic,
the Sheriff pins his tin star on the Town Drunk
and runs to catch the last stagecoach for California.

Meanwhile into a sunny plaza ghostly with fountains
here come generalizations in full dress uniforms,
all lavish in polished leather and brass buttons, tilting,
nearly top-heavy with medals, these brilliant officers
of the old regime. *Oompah-oompah-oompah* blares a band

while the crowds wolf down bananas and chocolate bars,
buy every balloon, and pound palms raw with sweaty applause.

Now cut directly to the inevitable moment
when the smoke is finally clearing away and there they are,
heels up and spurs down, those generalizations,
hanging conventionally from the streetlamps and phone poles.

Their rows of medals make a tinkly music.
See also, flat as oriental rugs along the street,
those are abstractions who once were fast on the draw.
While buzzards circle like homesick punctuation marks,
the simple and specific common nouns come forth again
to clean up the mess and mark the spot for scholars
    (oh oompah-oompah, chinka-chink)
with a row of gravestones grinning like false teeth.

To a Certain Critic

    from "Flashcards"

Walking in the woods, you turn over a rotten log.
Out from under crawls something very snotlike and pale.
If it could open its mouth and talk good English,
you'd know exactly what you sound like to me.

Two Elegies

1. Days of Our Lives Lie in Fragments

    in Memory of O. B. Hardison, Jr.

A calm clear morning on the York River
that we have both known and plied together;
a calm day and cool with the first touch

of autumn abroad, with geese at dawn
flying high and south in ragged formations
over the rocky shoreline lit by a rising sun.

Hours later in my boathouse, alone,
thinking about you and your sudden death,
I listen to a grayback gull perched on a piling,

cry out sounds that surely must be
an entirely incongruous laughter.
Tide turning; days of our lives lie in fragments.

There's no plot here, no narrative to follow,
a cold familiar voice whispers in my ear. I have
no reply, though I hope for something different, better.

Think how they slip away one at a time,
out of the light of all our ambiguous loves
and into the blaze and bright of another weather.

And soon, soon enough, we shall all cross over
out of these shadowy seasons of sooner and later,
each alone as can be with pain and sorrow.

See how, splendid as geese in flight,
they now join hands to move in a dance
to a music we cannot hear, can only guess at.

And I think I can see you there among the dancers
and I suddenly guess the music is the laughter
of angels, citizens of incredible ever-after.

Something wakes me, makes me step to the window:
tide running out, the river on fire with the sunset
and gulls overhead, white wings riding the wind.

2. *Tide Turning*

for John Ciardi

Even as, inch by living inch,
I contrive to chip and cut and carve
myself into various and sundry parts—

first, of course, the fingers
and the toes, then ears and nose,
these offered, as it were, in the words

of *The Book of Common Prayer,* to be
"a reasonable, holy and living sacrifice."
Eyes before sex, arms before legs;

next the thin peeled skin and last
the bloody mess of muscles and meat,
fat and lonely internal organs . . .

Must we be universal donors, John?

Much too much to hope for.
Better (and you knew it and said so,
so well and so many times)

to spend our skin and bones, to pay
out blood and breath upon
a wholly unimportant poem,

something reasonably simple and simply
(while memory burns) unforgettable:
you and I, one time, late on my front porch

in York Harbor, Maine, drinking
stone fences—your special favorite
apple jack and apple cider, all

the fumes and essences of Eden;
two old guys feeling no pain
underneath the brightly reeling stars,

while nearby, shiny and smooth
as a blacksnake, the river is rising
to high tide, inch by living inch.

March 1994

three poems for Cork Smith

Good As a Gold Watch
Something to see,
something really to behold:
how, sudden and graceful,
that redwing blackbird
can and does now light
on the tip of a cattail
and can ride with it,
rock and roll with it,
then steady (tick and tock)
keep time in empty air.

First Bluejay
Rain beading on buds of dogwood,
glistening, too, on first thrusts
of daffodils and crocus
like the shine of light on bayonets,
and here he comes now, the early
courtier of light and air, big boy
strutting his colors of blue and white,
daring the sky to cast off its gray cloak,
betting the trees will raise their hands
again in green and bright surrender.

Crows

Lord, but I do dearly love
these, your large, slow, reedy messengers,
your spies clad in shiny feathers,
sentinels of high places squawking
and cawing our arrivals and departures,
raggedy fliers rising in black caucus
or, grounded, the shifty epitome
of pure swagger and bravado.
Old crows, noisy flock,
we came through bad weather together
when all the trees were a cruel glitter
of ice and earth was a hardhearted stranger
who wished only catastrophe upon us,
you and I, shabby and insufferably proud,
perched here to witness the robins return.

FIGURE OF SPEECH

> It's a doggie dog world.
> —student paper

For years my litter of wounds
moved quietly, obedient and gentle,
well trained, eager to please.
Loved my quick heels and the tight leash,
begged cutely, fetched and rolled over,
and licked the fingers that fed them.

Now they return, a gaunt and feral pack,
each and every one presenting
a noisy mouth, rich with cruel teeth
and drooling tongue. See their red eyes,
how the hair stands up as they turn against
each other, killing for my choicest parts.

A Latin Epigram by Thomas More

When our prince is true and good,
He is the dog who guards the flock,
But when he is false, he turns into
The wolf who takes us for his food.

Some Enormous Surprises

Not many may now remember,
fewer and fewer remember,
most because they never knew
in the first place, being lucky
and too young, and others
because they are too few and too old
already; but anyway, I remember

the three reasons most often advanced
in those innocent days before the War
as strong and self-evident argument
that Adolph Hitler was crazy:
First, that he was a strict vegetarian.
Second, that he did not smoke or permit
any smoking around him, being convinced

that smoking cigarettes was somehow
linked to lung cancer.
Third, because he went around saying
that the Volkswagen, laughable beetle,
was the car of the future.
Maybe God, in all his power and majesty,
can still enjoy the irony of it.

Miles later, young man, old soldier, I
stand at the bar of a *gasthaus*
in Leonding, a country village near Linz,

lean against the dark, smooth, polished wood,
drinking and listening to very old men
remember the days of the Austro-Hungarian Empire.
Happens that Hitler's father lived here then.

And they can remember him and his son, too,
who every evening came to this *gasthaus*
for a bucket of beer for his father's supper.
Would stand there patiently waiting where
you are standing now, then, pail in hand,
set off under the early stars along a lane
toward the lights of home, whistling in the dark.

Everyone who knew agrees that then and later
he was a wonderful whistler, worth listening to.
I lean back against the bar to picture
how he was then, lips puckered,
whistling tunes I do not know,
beer rich and foamy, sloshing in the pail,
smell of woodsmoke, cooking meat and cabbage.

And, invisible and implacable, always
the wide smile of God upon His creatures, one and all,
great and small, among them this little pale-faced boy,
for whom He has arranged some enormous surprises,
beyond any kind of imagining, even myself,
drunk in this place, years from home, imagining it.

ANTHOLOGIES I (THEN AND THERE)

Not only the pleasures of dust,
of dry, stained pages and the out-of-date
card that proves nobody has even checked
this one out in a decade and not more
than half a dozen times in my whole lifetime.
RUTH HERSCHBERGER...LLOYD FRANKENBERG...

ALFRED HAYES . . . COMAN LEAVENWORTH . . . JOHN
THOMPSON, JR. . . .

But also all of these names and so many
more, not really forgotten, but not to be found,
either, anywhere else but here in the stacks
on shelves where Robinson's darkest inches
preserve the anonymous dignity of the unfamous.
MARYA ZATURENSKA . . . CALE YOUNG RICE . . .
H. PHELPS PUTNAM . . . WILLIAM ELLERY LEONARD . . .
ALFRED KREYMBORG . . .

And one great secret is simply this—how, taken
together, cheek-by-jowl, these people, these poets,
are often so much alike in form and substance
and more democratic in excellence and virtue
than anyone might have otherwise imagined.
                              MADELINE GLEASON . . .
ROBERT HORAN . . . MYRON O'HIGGINS . . . BYRON
VAZAKAS . . .

Years ago in the Village at the San Remo
I bought poems from Maxwell Bodenheim
at fifty cents a pop. Once at the Museum
of Modern Art I watched W. H. Auden unsuccessfully
try to check a bottle of champagne like a coat.
                    HELEN ADAM . . . EBBE BORREGAARD . . .
ADAM DRINAN . . . ELDER OLSON . . . MURRAY
NOSS . . .

But what of all the unfamous others, ourselves
I mean, still alive and on fire and in love
with the taste of words and the making of poems?
Who will come here to blow the dust away
and disturb the peace and oblivion we have earned?
                    FRED CHAPPELL . . . KELLY CHERRY . . .
R. H. W. DILLARD . . . BRENDAN GALVIN . . . GEORGE
GARRETT . . . DAVID SLAVITT . . . HENRY TAYLOR . . .

ANTHOLOGIES II (HERE AND NOW)

In this fat book I find
the signature, my own, my name
done in my same hand but different.
I could not make it that way now.

Summer of 1947 it would have to be.
The copyright is dated 1946—
A Little Treasury of Modern Poetry:
The Best Poems of the 20th Century.

A bit early then, wouldn't you say?
with this bloody century not yet half done
to be collecting and publishing the best.
Not at that time when everything was new

and wonderful, when so many of these poets,
words on pages, their pictures in the back,
were new names to me and even now
look younger than any of us ever were.

Day Lewis, Eberhart, George Barker
and John Manifold are purely and simply
smiling and now are sure enough dead
or dying. The others look deadly serious.

And all but a precious few of them
are long gone to glory or oblivion.
Does anyone alive still miss Gene Derwood
with those wild eyes and that funny hat?

Does anybody else but myself and Mary Lee
Settle still march to Manifold's "Fife Tune"?
Is anyone around to rejoice at the rhymes
of Hildegarde Flanner's "Noon On Alameda Street"?

The child who believed he was a man
and scribbled my name in the flyleaf here

went forth like Ransom's "Captain Carpenter"
to read his way through the book of wounds.

And this book sitting on its dark shelf
for years, a buried treasure of shining words,
a safe house assigned to all the dead poets
he loved and cherished at first sight.

DAVID R. SLAVITT

Ride the High Country

1

The long red underwear of Randolph Scott,
the gold-rimmed spectacles of Joel McCrea,
underscore age, and through the reverend plot
the old gunfighters ride for one more day.

And Ladd was old in *Shane,* and in *High Noon*
old Coop had all his wrinkles emphasized
(with visible distaste he drew his gun).
The ritual of honor is disguised

and is an act of memory and will.
The pistol-packing, popcorn-eating child
feels the pretended stubble on his chin
and imagines his bones weary after the kill.
Even the movies' West is no longer wild,
its *virtu* now a trail bum, a has-been.

2

Odysseus, safe at home, can be our friend.
Orestes and the Furies come to terms
—our terms: we, craven, crave the tamest end,
the fireside remembrances of storms,

the hero's diminution. The old hand
is slower on the draw, the eyes are gone.
We may admire, but we understand
that nerve is all McCrea is working on,

that aged manliness becomes absurd.
He makes mistakes out on the trail, he has
fallen into their obvious trap, is hit,
and crumples with gun blazing. On the hard
ground he shakes our comfort as he dies,
affirming the agelessness of what is fit.

Epitaph for Goliath

After so many victories, one
defeat, and that one by a stone:
but let this stone atone for that
breach of the order of combat.
He was a victim of a ruse
of the rude boy of the barbarous Jews.
Goliath shall have honor while
men yet have any use for style
or the purity of form they mean
by the accolade of Philistine.

Elegy for Walter Stone

> In August of 1959, I interviewed John Hall Wheelock
> at his home in Easthampton, N.Y., on the occasion of
> the publication of *Poets of Today VI,* which Mr.
> Wheelock edited and which included the poetry of
> Messrs. Gene Baro, Donald Finkel, and Walter Stone.

1

In the Apache over Hempstead with Finkel's view
of Fuji and the great wave in my hand . . .
But who would pretend to care? And why should Finkel
(not this particular Finkel, but any Finkel)
have a view of Fuji?
                              So I wondered whether
there was a first-rate delicatessen in all Japan.
An odd business this—when the mind takes off
leaving the body's ground, and the old terrain
with height is suddenly strange and unfamiliar,
when woods are smoothed to shrubbery, to lawn,
to plain green as the U.S. on a map,
when a Fuji is smoothed to paint, and paint to print,
and a craggy Finkel to an anonymous voice.

And the last is worst.
                    In London, on a grant
to study Renaissance eschatology,
the late professor and poet Walter Stone
committed suicide: an actual man
ground to a sheaf of poems that follow Finkel's
and in their total commitment to aesthetics
go his one better, for somewhere, still, in hiding,
in Queens, or perhaps the Bronx, surreptitious, Finkel
munches pastrami on rye (and afterwards
his tongue hunts for the caraway seeds in the teeth),
giving less of a damn for Fuji than, even, I.
Vive le Finkel! Which is exactly the point.

But let me be honest, for I too am a poet,
and the poet, Stone, is survived by a poet, his wife,
Ruth. And by Finkel (not my conceit, but the real
Donald Finkel, who lives and teaches at Bard),
and by his former students,
                            and by three daughters
who ought to despise that rising, the lyric thrust
that can take a man up where he only guesses at Hempstead,
sees something important in a dead Japanese volcano,
writes—as Stone did—stanzas about a spider
so fine he forgets about his daughters and wife,
forgets even himself, and the piece of work
that a man is, speechless and on the earth.

2

Later: at night: remembering the plane
and the quick trip out to visit John Hall Wheelock.
We savored the horror of it on the porch
and then went in to lunch.
                          Hart Crane
I can understand. Jumping overboard
was, for him, the perfectly fitting gesture,
with all the grief of his failings as a man,
and still a passing insult to his readers

who cared for the wrong and expendable things.

                                        But Stone
envied the angels' monotonous excellence,
their tuning-fork perfection, their effortlessness,
and even perhaps their wings . . .

                                The weights of the world
he shrugged off him, as if in a moment of pique:
his shoes, for example, in rows on some closet floor;
and his family, and his automobile, and his hairbrush;
and Vassar College itself where the grass grows green
and the laundry washes two thousand bras a week.
The stupid stuff of the world . . .

                                He renounced it all,
or perhaps it was a kind of an embrace,
to become, after an unpleasant moment of choking
(or do you feel even that? Does the neck snap
like a pretzel stick and the life go out in an instant
without that terrible dwindling?), like a stone,
like a table, a part of that same dumb stuff
(with a frozen smile for the possible play on his name).
Not merely the notion of rest, but to be a part
of the created world, to rot, to change,
to become absolutely chemical, and godly:
this, perhaps, is more the poet's delusion,
fitting the paradoxical turn of the mind
that rejects itself by its own final thought.
Suddenly, there he was, as dead as a door,
and full of the same dignity as the door
in its wonderful knowledge of the real nature of substance.

Or did he wander off in that dark wood
to visit the *malebolges,* where they talk
in terza rima, suddenly convinced . . .
But no!
                        Next I'll be calling out the dolphins
and making him into a hapless youth.

                                        He died
taking his motive with him, and leaving us

to guess what his question was that had no answer,
and to think, with awe, of a man dead in his prime.

3

The plane banked to the left and suddenly landed
as gracefully as a sea bird on a rock,
and I stepped out into the forenoon sun
and the salt smell of the wind coming off the ocean,
and felt that slight irrational sense of relief
that the plane had made it all right, and I was standing
there, on the ground, waving to Mr. Wheelock
who had a cab there, waiting. He told me how
he had once refused to go up in a plane with Lindbergh,
and smiled and remarked on the weather as we rode.
Nineteenth century outside and eighteenth in,
his house stands on a rise with a grove of trees
around it. Seventy summers it has been
standing there, with no other house in view,
and seventy summers John Hall Wheelock has lived
through the rooms of his father's house, and over the lawns.
But it is not virtue:

some of the good die young,
and some live long, and life is a random thing,
and the bus careens indifferently up on the sidewalk,
and the lightning, witless, streaks down into the park,
and the virus floats on the universal air.
It is not virtue, but a lucky chance
to which we attach perhaps too much importance
(and how we despise any quitting while you're ahead).
Wheelock was calm about it—regretful, but calm—
as we talked of Walter Stone, and then moved on
to talk of poetry or old pewter,
but there is no changing of subject at seventy-three,
and all the time he talked in one gentle tone
of the various guises of the one same thing
that a man must learn to gaze at, more and more:
Stone dead, and the poems left behind,
and the poems he would leave himself, and the pewter

and the house his father left, and the afternoon
perceptibly giving way.

                       Never mind how,
and never mind even when. All death is nature's,
whether by germ in the blood or idea in the head,
or sudden mischance in the wasteful order of things.
Gaze fixedly at it, and the distinctions
disappear.

             An unintellectual sadness
and a dumb calm is all I can summon up
for Walter Stone, for Wheelock, for myself,
for the act of imagination in Finkel's Fuji—
for all these sparks struck off by the turning world.

Sestina for the Last Week of March

Suddenly the ground is flesh and yielding
as if one walked on a body, and air is breath
and the woods are full of delicate, naked ladies
who hide in bushes and beckon behind the trees
in all the tempting attitudes of abandon
of the famous streets of certain infamous cities.

Who has not heard the erotic promise of cities,
or walked in squares with the light abruptly yielding
to shadows of unimaginable abandon?
But here, in the daylight and fresh air, the breath
of gin hangs on the juniper, and trees
carefully pose themselves like elegant ladies

considering some indiscretion. Ladies
learn to conceal such thoughts in civilized cities.
Oh, sometimes, in a formal park, the trees
will make their improper suggestions, conversation yielding
to difficult silences, the very drawing of breath
becoming absurdly physical: "Abandon

pretense, civilization, cities. Abandon
all the constraints by which you live as ladies.
Strip naked, lie in the grass, pick baby's breath
bouquets, and flee for your lives, flee the cities. . . ."
But they never do. That week of spring yielding
yields itself to summer. Leaves clothe the trees.

And yet, some must have gone. Behind the trees,
those delicate creatures of our fancy's abandon
must have begun somewhere. There are myths yielding
many examples—reasonable ladies
of the kind one meets in fashionable cities
once, in the woods, struggled to catch their breath

and changed in the time it takes to draw a breath,
turning into, melting into trees.
Their stories are embroidered back in the cities,
tamed for us who can bear only so much abandon.
They have been refined, no doubt for the sake of the ladies
who know their truth and long for such a yielding

and for gentlemen of the cities, lest they abandon
fine careers, fine ladies, and run off, yielding
to the whispered breath of nymphs, behind the trees.

Le Babouinisme

We hung in trees once, and small boys will still
scramble up easy apples and eye the tall
oaks and elms. Our legend of the fall
goes back to that old grove we swarmed until
some tempting possibility on the plain
lured us down. With our opposing thumb,
we hefted a dead branch; we had become
hunters with clubs; and somewhere in the brain
a memory persists, lofty, leafy,

so that we, on a walk now, in a furtive hour,
look up to green sanctuaries, escape
our guilt for a while, and try to imagine beefy
baboons, gentle with vegetarian power,
secure in their grip on a joy we barely ape.

NIGHT CREATURES

Imagine imagination that varies inversely
with being, so that elephants must lack it,
barely able to grasp their own bulk and weight
as they must be also deficient in deviousness,
thinking in straight lines from which they scarcely
waver, hacking trails of vectors with racket
they hardly notice, bulling toward a mate. . . .
We must be cleverer, think more, being less,
who, to scamper from cover, must risk our lives,
touch only briefly, but dream and remember long,
like mice, like voles, those brave fools of the night
all men with mistresses become, whose wives
trumpet the truth: that we are small and wrong
and hopeless, and they are angry, huge, and right.

NURSERY RIME

for Joshua

bo
peep
little bo peep
little old bittle old o bo peep

old bo peep
little bo peep
little ittle bo pittle ittle o peep

DAVID R. SLAVITT

o o peep
little old peep
bittle ittle odle ittle o bittle peep bo
odle ittle peep bo
little bo peep

hey diddle diddle and a little bo peep
little bo diddle hey little bo peep
fiddle faddle peep hey
bo bo peep hey
little diddle he pay
heap peep peep

bo
peep
little bo peep
had a little ho ho
goodbye peep

THE DEATH OF MOZART

Uremia is painful enough without birds
chirping their heads off, warbling in thirds
while you're busy dying. A little quiet, please.
I want no canary around for my decease.
No more did he. But still, it is bothersome
to think that when his final hour had come
Mozart sent his canary away. Did the bird
make mistakes? sing badly what Mozart heard
in his mind's ear, following a score
of canary music? Or, did the bird soar
on aviary arias, a strain
so fine that he beat time with throbs of pain?
Or worse, did the bird's song suggest a measure
there was no more time for, now, so that the pleasure
of composing turned to the pain of holding a flood,
as the body held the urine in the blood?

I fear the worst, that Mozart, as you or I,
just wanted quiet, quiet in which to die,
unbroken by any sound but his own breath.
With the bird gone, he had quiet. Which was death.

HOMAGE TO LUIGI BOCCHERINI

1

Landon to Haydn's Roosevelt, Luigi
Boccherini also ran
                              bows over strings
made minor music poor (I mean unmoneyed)
and died poor.

Melody, child of a pennywhistle mind,
brings out the warbler in us, chirruping sparrow,
the color of jays, gay and gliding:
all laud and honor then from the dancing dons
who whistle across the court, and pay ye all homage
to Boccherini and his singing like.

Not the common man; not great, nor near great,
nor "for trying" but *ipse,* good as he was,
musician, music (i.e., of the muse),
and in that thrall—like to a priesthood,
                                        like to a disease . . .
That mind could pulse the heartbeat, fleshed and ringing,
praise Boccherini, awful and abstract.

2

I have heard that agile playing
in drowsy claret afternoons,
poised upon some fragile word
of mine, or drifting on his tunes,
and loved as he was close to me

and trembled at his violin.
Boccherini, peerless, plays
the dancing shadows' coming in.

3

"Poet, make up your miracles, work your wonders:
that epic sop: tell him your blood is his:
journey: blind, crazy, clubfoot, or drunk:
harrow again, or climb the mountain and ask

What world is this of yours? what thing this music?

and make him speak as you have found him out."

But intervals of voices in the hearing,
in the world's hearing, faint as they were, are
(as, say, a small saint's obscure passion)
                                        his
and done for the doing, favor or heaven, or no.
Then let him alone, you; he could give over
this and the next world, and without such questions,

and as you fear his music, fear him, praise
and, silent, hallow Boccherini, dead.

The Calf and the Ox

(XXXVI—The Fables of Avianus)

Scampering the pasture, that's how now,
the brown cow, a calf still, sees
in the next field, yoked to a heavy plow,
the dumb ox, and stops to shoot the breeze:
"What's that contraption? What kind of life
is that?" The questions, even the mocking laugh
get no rise from the ox, but a silent stare

at the farmer who carries a glittering butcher knife
and a light halter, coming toward the calf.
Nobody gets to choose which yoke to wear.

Three from *Dozens*

52

"Whether clever or stupid, those beautiful young
men and women, bound for the tennis courts,
are surely ignorant, having suffered or lost
nothing." The coronel's point? That only torture,
whether from nature or human nature, elicits
truth and turns evasive minds to face
demanding questions. He calls his secret police
midwives to truth, regrets the labor pains,
shrugs, falls silent, stares at his shiny boots.
The refuge of our frivolous verandah,
precious, fragile as crystal, is permitted
as doctors permit their terminal patients dope.

83

The dignity of politics? The coronel
produces a very expensive fountain pen
from somewhere in his tunic, holds it up,
and asks what it can do. "A doctor, a judge,
or a general can kill with it, but a dentist
is a figure of fun because he seldom risks
his patients' lives. In times of peace and plenty,
politics also is trivial, but now . . ."
He unscrews the cap, stares at the broad gold nib,
and with a lethal flourish signs his bar chit.
"The crocodile, most of the time, is sleeping,
but when he wakes, there is sudden beautiful silence."

142

These pigeons survive where tough crows can't, dance
through traffic, beg, steal, crafty as gulls
or crude jays. The trick is seeing the sense
in pediment and cornice, merging with soot,
and being able to eat garbage, Twinkies,
kernels in horseshit. Most of us are awkward
seabirds that take a mile of ungainly running
to get ourselves airborne, and land hard.
Okay in the Keys or the Caribbean,
but not here. You got to learn street smarts.
Pay attention, birdbrain: know how to dart
down for sustenance, up for safety, and fast.

THE ELM

Late-leafing, as if shy,
it was pleased, nevertheless, to strike its best
pose against the western sky;
but that last elm is diseased, my children tell me,
and its branches die

as if touched in June, in May,
by a bite of killing frost from an autumn still
theoretical to summer people. They
can't understand it. I couldn't either, but
having gone away,

I've lost the feel of the year,
its times and seasons, jumbled them up, as that tree
has, so that quince will appear
to bloom with the hawthorn, the burning bush, and all
at once. It's queer

how nature contrives to mock
one's frailties. So Adam, hearing word
      of the death of something he'd known in Eden—the roc,
dodo, or dinosaur—would feel . . . Sadness?
      Triumph? Or shock?

      Not having the right to grief
or ground for any other coherent feeling,
      I can see each starving yellowed leaf
falling to leave a scar against the sunset,
      like a cross for a thief.

TITANIC

Who does not love the *Titanic?*
If they sold passage tomorrow for that same crossing,
who would not buy?

To go down . . . We all go down, mostly
alone. But with crowds of people, friends, servants,
well fed, with music, with lights! Ah!

And the world, shocked, mourns, as it ought to do
and almost never does. There will be the books and movies
to remind our grandchildren who we were
and how we died, and give them a good cry.

Not so bad, after all. The cold
water is anaesthetic and very quick.
The cries on all sides must be a comfort.

We all go: only a few, first-class.

BLOODY MURDER

Beauty and truth may dally together,
but when it comes time to pop the question,
it's ugliness that settles in
to take the vows with truth for the long
haul, the enduring and faithful companion.
The difficult lesson we all must study
is how to be children of such a marriage
and honor what we cannot love.

After the burglar bludgeoned my mother
to death with a bathroom scale and a large
bottle of Listerine, the police
recommended Ronny Reliable's
Cleaning Service—one of a growing
number of firms that make it their business
to clean up after messy murders,
suicides, and other disasters.

They have the solvents and strong stomachs
for such work. I still wonder
who would choose that kind of employment
or what the men who performed this awful
and intimate task looked like. We only
spoke on the phone; detectives let them
in; and the charge showed up on my next
Mastercard bill. But I know they were there.

The chemical smell hung in the air
of the empty house for nearly a month,
proving they'd been there and done the job,
which is to say that the other unthinkable
thing had happened first. Excess,
whether of pleasure or pain, beggars
belief so that lovers and mourners rub
their eyes in similar ways, trying
to take in the thought along with the image.

One needs both. On the KLH
radio my mother kept on
top of the bureau, there was a white
electric cord the assiduous workers
missed with its evidence a doubting
Thomas needs or dares, to challenge
nerve and love, the reliquary
stain of what had been done and undone.

It wasn't a bouillon cube, would not
reconstitute in heat and water,
but there it was, to be faced, the mark
of faceless functionaries, furies,
or Ronny Reliable's Cleaning Service.
Jesus knew how it was—and wasn't—
a comfort to tell his stunned disciples:
this is my body, this is my blood.

PLODDERS

Consider the unclever. I
envy them rather. They do not try

but dimly rouse themselves to their half-
wakefulness. They never laugh,

say clever things, or write them. Stolid,
earnest, sober, very solid,

they go about their jobs and lives.
We are the ones who, sharp as knives,

have to worry lest we lose
our edges. They don't. Like old shoes,

they're comfy, good for years of service.
(We're unreliable and nervous.)

They are, on the whole, a happy crew.
I envy them. (I envy you.)

FORIO

German tourists now come for the mud,
the brownish water in pools from the hot springs,
their peculiar cheese-and-bologna breakfasts, and one
another. Auden, were he somehow to return,

would be distressed, but then distress would be
familiar and what the Mezzogiorno means,
what Ischia anyway meant. The people were mean,
poisoned one of his cats, and cheated him more

even than vague and preoccupied English poets
ought to expect. The island, nevertheless,
has pleasant wines and, at Forio, a prospect
of water one way and Mount Epomeo

looming the other (with buggery and sunshine
at bargain rates Inglesi delight in). What
more could a man want? He toddled down
the hill on his tender feet to inspect the monsters—

contorted heaps of lava the old volcano
had spat into the sea—to buy a paper,
and have a coffee or perhaps an aperitivo
before he trudged back. He wanted only

what most writers want—to be left alone,
but the children teased him, as even these poor
kids will, an odd enough duck. His *"Basta!"*
was the victory they'd get before they let him

go. That he could, leaving, bless the region
shows his generous nature, or perhaps his modest
expectations. The name of his street is changed,
and nobody here remembers an English poet.

Not even the workmen, affixing one end of the frame
for the colored lights they dearly love for the feast
of one of those "minim saints" to Auden's house,
know who lived inside. Still he has joined

his list of "sacred meridian names—Vico,
Verga, Pirandello, Bernini, Bellini,"
and those gods who arrange such matters have contrived
that the decorations attach to the proper building.

History of My Ear

for Brendan Galvin

1

I sported badges of bloody campaigns such as no
implausible generalissimo ever would wear.
My recruit's first pip, hidden away, was almost
forgotten—but that's another story. Parades,
when peace breaks out, degenerate to charades,
and the martial music turns tinny. Bystanders
jeer and call out advice on where to stick it—
in your ear, of course. Hamlet's father ought
to have taken better care, to have given or lent
ear to that buzzing at one of the seven gates.

2

To turn a deaf ear, you have to have one.
With my good side on the pillow, I could sleep
like a baby, but then I was a baby. My nights
are rougher now—the racket comes from inside.

There's nothing to hope for. The quiet I have already
tasted will soon enough extend itself,
as if I had lain all those years on that narrow
patch where the back-hoe will come to chuff
and scoop the sod for me, that good ear
to the ground like an Indian's, listening for hoofbeats.

3

Ingmar Bergman says that there are only
two kinds of films: the documentary . . . (And?
Musicals?) Almost! "Dreams" is what he calls them,
whether a hundred showgirls tap-dance on white
pianos or the business is rather grimmer.
The right was my documentary ear; my left
was what was left, the way for another music
to conceive itself in intervals between
louder events. The better the fountain pen
the smoother its nib, and the closer to perfect silence.

4

Children daydream, romp in recesses, hide
and seek, as they play, trying on and out
those dreams of life that may come true, dog them,
come to heel, or snap at their heels. But later
such respites turn on them and spite them. The hard
lesson the hard of hearing learn is retreat
from attention to conversation. One gives up
and sinks into that shred of baby-blanket
silence he has never wholly abandoned,
by now a ratty rag, black as a shroud.

5

The Oticon devices have nothing to do
with the scourge, but we worry, nevertheless, that these
aids intrude the world upon us, so it
becomes, as a retrovirus does, us,
or what was encoded as us but is now that ruin
a self would resist if any self were left.

The mute key on the TV control is a clumsy
substitute: one forgets, and commercials blare
while the virgin nerve the broken drum protected
thrills to be learning the other's whorish tricks.

6

The center shifts. The sensation in the normal
ear, which is used to doing all the work,
is of deprivation. To share is to be deprived.
The dumb brain in its box tries to work it out—
if the sounds are equal, it must mean they are loud
but something is wrong with the right ear, and I yawn,
knowing better, to clear the eustachian tube
that isn't clogged. They say it will take time
to unlearn fifty years of lessons. In heaven,
how long does it take to forget how not to fly?

7

Tiresias may be patron of blindness, but who
speaks to the deaf (or shouts at the hard of hearing)?
Evelyn Waugh, who affected an old ear trumpet
until some bright young Mayfair mayfly poured
most of her martini into it . . . ? Nasty!
They made them with sherry then. Beethoven, surely,
whose music, after he loses his hearing, becomes
increasingly cerebral. From deep wellsprings
it oozes up, thick and black, from levels
of silence only bad ears ever fathom.

8

It teaches patience, attention, and how to read
the meaning of moving lips, or on those faces
where the lips are set, the mood the eyes betray.
Inward, that concentration reaches to treasures
monsters guard. A poet's ear can hear
what dead voices whisper, nursery jingles
and lullabies a part of him still intones,
observant as any monk. To take these vows

is only a start; he then must wait for the world
to hush, fall to its knees, and join in prayer.

9

That it doesn't breaks his heart, even though he knew
from the start how absurd an idea it was. What child,
having done well, will not look up to the beaming
sun of his parents' praise in which to bask?
He is not proud of himself but of the rare
gift he was given, and from which he has given
everything. That nobody cares is the last
hard lesson it takes almost as long
to master as the craft. Another silence,
he greets it as he would a familiar, a friend.

10

What sounds do the stars make, or our cells,
dreaming themselves into being and burning fires
that rage or gutter and die? That there can be
poems changes the stillness. Think of a phone,
that at any moment could ring, that waits to ring
in a silence therefore different, leaning into
the future. In such moments of eerie quiet,
as between a lightning bolt and thunderclap,
one learns to live. The air tingles, the whole
body strains to hear. . . . I am all ears.

CROSSROADS

for Vera

A lowering sky, a wide expanse of stubble
in empty fields, and two roads crossing where
the village houses, leaning together, huddle
    against cold Polish air:

I see that dour landscape clearly, although
I've never been there. It could be from a story
we tell to children—but then, on second thought, no.
    Why should we have them worry

as we do? Nothing remains of that crossroads
hamlet. One street, I'm told, had the better houses;
the other was where we lived, of course, but those
    gaps close as the time passes.

It was for our sake our grandparents gave it up
and left the place, things, people they belonged to
for the dream of somewhere safer. On the trip
    that thought was what they clung to

for dear life, and, alive, I'm glad they came,
but what they abandoned is what I dream of now,
asleep, while people who don't even know my name
    monitor consoles that show

what zones in my house have been violated—what doors
or windows opened, or motion sensors tripped
by the cat or some intruder. On the street, cars
    are stolen and stripped

by desperate men, wild children. . . . Who can say?
It isn't safe here, or anywhere, and God,
stunned, still mourns at that crossroads, far away,
    where also the dream died

of the Socialists. (The Zionists' went later.)
Over those empty fields, the wind's low moan
keens for those who died there together better
    than we die here alone.

The Gig

On a tippy table, here at the Penn State Days
Inn, I've been scribbling, mostly to pass the time. . . .
It's hardly what those would-be M.F.A.s
imagine, or want to do, who think that I'm

curmudgeonly, or frivolous, or tired,
and resent being discouraged. And what if they do
get published and, on the strength of that, are hired
to teach creative writing (and one or two

sections of bonehead English)? Will I owe
apologies? Or will they also come
to such a pass and room as this and know
envy, resentment, and, worst of all, the numb

indifference that conspires with our own distaste
for readings in ugly lecture halls to sad
small groups, like all the others that we've faced,
impassive, if not sullen, ill read, ill clad,

as their instructors are, who never smile
or even get the jokes but talk of deals,
and publishers, and resent displays of style?
Why condescend to do it, then, if it feels

so bad, and worse all the time? One owes it to
the work? Of course not! But necessity
sneaks up from behind to bite you: you come through
to help a son with dentist's bills that he

can't manage. Therefore, I contrive a grin
with my own expensive teeth. I'll do my show-
and-tell and then get through the party in
my honor. Checking again the impossibly slow

minute hand of my watch, I'll long to get back
to this Days Inn and to quiet—my natural

habitat. Both flattery and attack
I shall endure with an abstract rictus and all

the grace I can muster, keeping my mouth shut,
for there's nothing to say, so long as they're hoping for
tricks of the trade—there are no tricks, and it's not
a trade. Imagine silence. A page turns. More

silence and that's it. That's all there is.
And yet, from beyond the lamp's charmed circle, faces
are peering, the garish light of the lit biz
having lured them from their usual hiding places.

They're hungry for my secrets? Unearned income
is the most important; then, to have griefs like mine
for which there is no cure, though there can be some
respite with pen and paper's anodyne.

That's not what they want, is surely too much to handle,
but all I have, a gift not of my choosing,
and if no one seems to think it worth the candle
to learn to write well just to be amusing,

there's no help for them, or hope for their poems and
stories, those recitations, thinly disguised,
of betrayals they've suffered from parent or boyfriend
behaving badly. I was not surprised

by any trope or image of theirs. Then why
do they persist? What is the use? They are sad
poster children for some disease you and I
have never heard of. They have got it bad,

but I do, too, I suppose, am a chronic case,
no longer contagious, but that is what confuses
or even annoys. Too bad, but I'll leave this place
with a check for my son—worth a few new bruises.

Assume a God

from *A Gift: The Life of da Ponte*

Assume a god, or a set of them,
playful or mean, who toy with us.
What is the worst they can do
to our Lorenzo?
                  Put on *Una cosa rara*
in London and have it succeed.
Let them admire da Ponte
now that he's out of the way.
                      Put on Mozart,
La clemenza di Tito first, and *Die Zauberflöte*
(done in Italian), and then, in 1811,
                             Così fan tutte.
Figaro the following year.
Da Ponte thousands of miles away, has no idea,
might as well be as dead as Mozart.

In 1817, *Don Giovanni* triumphs
in London,
which, for all it matters to him,
                        is China, the moon. . . .

That's never the point,
but then what is? Does it make
any difference?
Either way one answers,
the implications are dreadful.

If we suppose he was better than he knew,
that makes him a tool, a toy, and cozens him
of what any man deserves—
                      the fruits of his labor.

That black water he crosses
surges and falls back, in waves,

predictable tides, idiotic, relentless,
as if there were sense,
as if, with sufficient energy, one might
swim to some safe haven, reach dry land.

Psalm 34

Always, I shall bless my Lord,
Boast of His love, and demonstrate
Clearly to those who have not had
Deliverance from affliction the great

Easing He offers. Let us as one
Frame prayers of praise and thanks to Him.
God is more radiant than the sun.
His rays can penetrate to the dim

Interior places of the soul.
Just before we abandon hope,
Kind angels come, console, condole,
Lighting the dark through which we grope.

Magnificent! O taste and see!
Near at hand is abundant proof
Of the goodness of God. And happy are we
People who worship beneath His roof.

Quite awesome is He, and holy men
Revere and love Him, knowing He will
Save and protect them, confident when
They trust in Him, they may fear no ill.

Up on the veld, the lions' young
Voice in vain their hunger, but here
We are fed by the Lord. We wander among
Xeric wastes, and freshets appear.

Your faith may waver, but trust that His vast
Zig-zagging lines will converge at last.

WORRY BEADS

from "Desk Set"

The string of my worry beads
frayed, gave way. I had to have the beads
restrung—and have to worry now about the beads themselves,
which ought to have functioned as emblems
without assuming, without presuming. . . .
They impose themselves now as an independent subject
of worry: thirty-three beads and a marker bead.
They have some Islamic significance,
although I bought them in spite of that,
which is, I suppose, another reason to worry.
What does Islam know that the rest of us don't?
Are there only thirty-three worries? Are you hungry,
are you thirsty, are you cold, have you had a good bowel movement
    recently,
will you dream you are falling but, this time, not wake, actually hit,
    and die upon impact?
And so forth, for twenty-eight other categories of concern . . .
What sage or lunatic came to this abstruse reckoning? And was he
right? Was Spinoza right? Or Leibniz? (That can't be a worry!)
There must be a miscellaneous category, which enables
but also defeats the entire system. What if
my jeweler calls, tells me the beads are restrung,
and I go and get them, only to find that I have nothing left to worry
    about, and have wasted my money
having had them restrung? I pray
for a life in which that could be a legitimate source of worry.
I cannot imagine such a life, but I am already vertiginous with envy
of the protagonist of my sudden fiction. . . .
The worry beads are blue and white, irregular, and nicely

nubbly to the touch. It is comforting to flick them with one's thumb.
That's an answer, albeit not a sufficient one. But what was the question?
Ah, yes, Leibniz' first name—was Gottfried,
which is one less thing to worry about, except that I am likely to forget it,
which is deplorable but one of the consequences of getting older, and
    another, and slightly more serious subject for concern.

The Second Murderer

> *Clar.* In God's name, what art thou?
> *2nd Mur.* A man as you are.
> *Clar.* But not, as I am, royal.
> *2 Mur.* Nor you, as we are, loyal.
> —Shakespeare

People assume it's a rank. Second lieutenant?
Fiddler? Mate? Why not, therefore, a second
murderer . . . ? Plausible, but incorrect,
and the implications are misleading. There's no
exam I'd sit for to be promoted, no
august committee before which I'd have to appear
to get to be first murderer. That is a different
calling altogether. We are not like them,
not, if I may say, hotheaded, fanatic. . . . To be
neutral, let us call it *engagé*.
Your first murderer has a cause, an end
to justify his means. He cares, you see.
We are more balanced, reasonable people.
To us, it's a job, unpleasant perhaps, but jobs
often are. Your first murderer goes at it
with fervor in his heart, on principle.
We, less grandiose, are mostly after
profit, one way or another. Like most of you.
    Another misconception has us
second murderers not so much assistants

194

as bumblers, oafs—but if we were so inept,
why would they need us? And they do, indeed,
need our presence. Committed as he may be,
your first murderer's not an expert, requires
help, more often than not, to get the job done.
More important, a second murderer changes
him from an undistinguished killer and mere cutthroat
to a leader. Now, it's a project, an enterprise
with a mission statement, an organizational plan,
and all that fine administrative framework
to disguise, a little, the unattractive truth.
Why else risk taking a witness along?
It's not an excursion. Nobody ever says:
"I'm off to kill the Duke of Clarence. Join me?
And afterwards, perhaps a spot of supper . . . ?"
Nevertheless, there is a social dimension,
a need he has for complicity, to share
that burden of guilt he'd otherwise bear himself.
I think it's a kind of marriage—for each of us, knowing
the other's secret, can bring him down. Joined now,
made kin to us by that blood we have shed together,
he knows he's never absolutely alone.
A danger, it's also a comfort, or was once. . . .
Now, with your Oswalds and your Sirhan Sirhans,
it doesn't cross their minds to recruit one of us.
Why? My guess for what it's worth is that guilt
has spread so wide that no assassin worries
in the night's dark moments lest he be the worst man
alive in the world. He's crazy, but not enough
to feel cut off from mankind—not these days.
I'm semiretired. But I still keep my beeper.

HENRY TAYLOR

THE HORSE SHOW AT MIDNIGHT

I The Rider

Now, the showground is quiet.
The spectators all have departed.
Along the walls of the arena
The jumps are lying, collapsed.
The moon shines down on the grandstand
As I walk out across the ring
Alone, watching for what may not be here.
I take my place as a judge
In the center of the ring, waiting.
Asleep in their stables, the horses
Awaken to my thought-out call
And rise from the straw and walk
To the ring, silently and formally.
One after another they march
Around the ring, proudly, like men.
I stand on my toes and speak softly—
They all start to gallop at once
Noiselessly, weightlessly,
Their hoofs beating only within me.
Around the ring, faster and faster,
Their manes like flame in the moonlight,
They gallop in single file,
Halt as I think the command,
Then walk out of the ring
Into darkness, proudly and softly.
One horse only stays with me
Straining to hear a command
That I am unable to utter.
On a sign from someone unseen
The jumps rise up into place
By themselves, hugely and suddenly.
The horse kneels down on the grass
And rises up with a rider.
As I watch from my place as a judge

My heart and my bones leave my body
And are heart and bones of this rider.
As the horse flies over the fences
The horseman whose heart is the judge's
Makes no movement or sound,
But the horse knows what he must do
And he takes the fences one by one
Not touching the poles or the ground.
At the end of the course he halts
And the fences retreat to the ringside,
Then my horse and his rider are gone.
Alone in the grandstand's shadow
I call to him time after time
But only my bones fill my body.
The rider and horse do not answer.
I walk across to the gate
Looking back once more at the ring
Watching for sound or a movement
Left behind by one horse that I love.
The empty ring does not echo
And the horse has left no hoofprints.
In the moonlight, alone, I sink down
Kneeling in nothing but bones
And I call to my horse once again
But the ring and the grandstand are quiet.

II *The Horse*

In the darkened stable I move in my sleep
And my hoof stirs the straw and wakes me.
I rise, breathing softly, inhaling
The moonlight outside like perfume,
Straining to hear the command
That moved my hoof in the straw.
In my huge, shining shape I stand
Listening, and I hear the calling again.
Through the locked door of my stall,
Obeying, I march to the show ring,

Beside horses I cannot see, but feel
As their hoofs shake the air around me.
I march to the sound of a heart
That beats somewhere just ahead of me.
In the ring I lead a parade
In a circle, galloping and galloping,
And I wait for a change in the heartbeat.
I halt, and the others march out,
And I sink to my knees on the grass
As a body gets up on my back
And the man in the ring disappears.
I rise to my feet once again
And look around me at fences
Which have sprung like trees from the ground.
My shape fills the air as I fly
Over boards, stone walls, and poles,
And the bones on my back do not move.
Still I move to the beat of a heart
That brought me out of the stable.
I stop when I clear the last fence,
And the bones dismount, and I march
From the ring to the sound of the heart.
Back in my stable I lie down
Wide-eyed, breathless and shining,
Still hearing within me the call
That brought me over the jumps.
This time I cannot obey:
This man is only partly a rider
And the rider in him is within me.
Helpless, grief-stricken, and alone,
He kneels out there in the moonlight
With only his bones for a body,
His heart singing deeply within
A shape that moves with new life.
I believe in the singing, and sleep.

Breakings

Long before I first left home, my father
tried to teach me horses, land, and sky,
to show me how his kind of work was done.
I studied how to be my father's son,
but all I learned was, when the wicked die,
they ride combines through barley forever.

Every summer I hated my father
as I drove hot horses through dusty grass;
and so I broke with him, and left the farm
for other work, where unfamiliar weather
broke on my head an unexpected storm
and things I had not studied came to pass.

So nothing changes, nothing stays the same,
and I have returned from a broken home
alone, to ask for a job breaking horses.
I watch a colt on a longe line making
tracks in dust, and think of the kinds of breakings
there are, and the kinds of restraining forces.

An Afternoon of Pocket Billiards

Here where there is neither hope nor haste
all my days blend; each dark day is misplaced
      inside my crowded head.
I try to beat a game, half chance, half cold
and steady practice, struggling for the skill
that might kill chance. But chance's claws take hold,
the game is wrecked, and time is all I kill:
no sleight of hand or heart can overcome
the fear that, in this darkness, only time
      is not already dead.

I narrow down my gaze to where I waste
days growing used to a dusty taste
        that hangs in the dead air;
motes of chalk and talcum powder sift
down past the hard edge of the swinging light
above my table. Jukebox voices drift
by me through the dark, raveled with a slight
vibration from that older world beyond
the window: now I listen for a sound
        that may still rise somewhere

        this afternoon, away
from here . . . my eyes wander from where I play
to the motions of more skillful hands than mine:
another player leans above his cue.
Between us, those old tremors seem to move
the air I stare through, almost as if you
were breathing here: that half-remembered love
        obscures the perfect shot
I turned to watch; I turn back, but am caught
between my past and the shifting design

on a green field of order where I wait
for time and strength of will to dissipate
        these shapes that coil and turn
above the hush and click of herded spheres.
Brief glimpses of a chain of treacheries
flicker around a melody that bears
into this room the gradual disease
we fled when you tore blindly out our driveway
for the last time, and I came here to play,
        to wait for your return,

for this game's random shifts to bring you back
or set me free. As I blunder through each rack,
        no two shots are the same;
yet if, beneath them all, dim certainties

evolve to hold my called shots on a course
that weaves beyond love's sudden vagaries,
still, an impulse like love, in the force
behind that wavering song, caroms my thought
into an old mistake: with every shot
      I call, I speak your name.

High and low, striped and solid balls rotate
in endless formations as time grows late.
      My concentration breaks
just at the dead-reckoned instant before
each shot: testing stroke and angle, I ease
down on the felt and line it up once more;
too late, I feel that slight vibration seize
my arm—too late to stand. My knocking heart
shatters skill and chance, and takes the game apart.
      I make my own mistakes.

I chalk my cue and call for one more rack,
believing I might still untwist the wreck
      your song makes in my head.
I think how spellbound Bottom woke to shout
through nightmare trees, "When my cue comes, call me,
and I will answer . . ." Your voice might find me out,
note by note unraveling to recall me
from this enchanted wood beyond your reach.
"When my cue comes . . ." Moving only by touch,
      I try to hold the thread,

listening for the words to an old song
that draws me down, sets me adrift among
      patterns below the game.
The words will not connect. Red blood and bone,
older than love, the swirling echo drives
me down below green felt toward solid stone
whose grains read out the sequence of my lives
in sounds like underwater footsteps. My blind

and whispering fingers stroke the stone to find
        strength to forget the shame

I learned too long ago. I may be wrong
to follow an ancient, dimly sounding song
        whose melody is fear,
whose words might never speak; but now I know
that in it, somewhere, forces of hand and will
combine like dancers on a stage. And now,
within the strictness of my touch, I feel
a surge of steadiness. I rise to air,
to dust and vacant noise and old despair.
        Error still holds me here,

        but I'll be right someday:
though one song of old love has died away,
an older song is falling into place.
From now on I will play to make it speak,
to see the form its words give to this game.
I see, as I move into another rack,
that all days in this cavern are the same:
        endless struggles to know
how cold skill and a force like love can flow
together in my veins, and be at peace.

Here where there is neither hope nor haste
I narrow down my gaze to where I waste
        this afternoon away;
on a green field of order, where I wait
for this game's random shifts to bring you back,
high and low, striped and solid balls rotate.
I chalk my cue and call for one more rack,
listening for the words to an old song
I learned too long ago: "I may be wrong,
        but I'll be right someday."

BUILDINGS AND GROUNDS

for Richard Dillard

The house we moved into has been landscaped
    so that it has the portable, plastic look
    of a Sears, Roebuck toy farm.

All up and down our street, the same minor artist seems
    to have been at work; our neighbors' lawns are
    watered and mowed truly until they are carpets,

their shrubs are lovingly trimmed and shaped
    into green velvet eggs and spheres.
    Our neighbors watch us like hawks,

wondering whether we have the equipment,
    the know-how, the spirit, to strive with them
    as they strive with their landscapes.

Oh, let me bring my home from the South to this street!
    I will let the grass grow until it is knee-high,

I will import chickens and a blue-tick hound to trample
    the grass and dig bone-holes and scratch-holes,

I will set up on cinderblocks in the front yard
    a '38 Ford with no tires or headlights,

I will sit in the gutted driver's seat
    with a bottle of Old Mr. Mac, glaring at my
    neighbors, reading aloud from *God's Little Acre*,

I will be a prophet of wildness and sloth!

But the Puritan gaze of my neighbors cuts through
    my desperate vision of home—my dream house
    will not flourish here.

I will spend my rapidly declining years
    reading the labels on bags of crabgrass killer,

pushing my lawn mower until my front yard
    is as smooth as a green on a golf course,

clipping and shaping my landlord's opulent shrubs.

But don't misunderstand me—I have not been
    converted; I will still make something
    to sustain me here in this alien land.

I will plant mint in the flowerbeds beside
    the Shasta daisies we brought from Monticello,

I will set up a croquet course on the front lawn
    with a slender drink-stand at each wicket
    to hold my frosty mint juleps,

I will station an iron jockey by the driveway
    to stare back into the pitiless eyes
    of my neighbors' pink plastic flamingoes,

I will keep a Tennessee Walking Horse in the garage
    and give him a foxhound for company,

I will stand out front in a white linen suit
    surveying my plantation,

I will plant a magnolia tree.

But now, at the height of my visionary ecstasy,
    the telephone rings. It is the man
    next door, calling to let me know

that my sprinkler is turned up too high
    and is sprinkling the seats of his convertible.

I go out to turn down the water, and I see
    that the cedar needs trimming again,
    that the elm twigs need to be raked.

I will do those things. I will hoe and trench
    and weed, I will mow the grass.
    I have moved in here now,

and I have to do what I can.

DE GUSTIBUS AIN'T WHAT DEY USED TO BE

> Poetry, like the old darky mowing
> the lawn, can't be hurried.
> —Marshall Fishwick

You have to know how to handle it.
Treated with understanding,
it is loyal, slow, and dependable,
with an earthy charm of its own.
    It walks into your life and sits down.

If it sometimes moves so sluggishly
that the grass grows up behind it
as fast as it's being cut,
you tell it to keep trying.
    It will not be hurried.

It shuffles and makes excuses
and tells you the mower is dull,
but you know better than that:
never trust it with machinery.
    It makes room for itself in your life.

It breaks everything it touches,
and steals what isn't nailed down;

its speech is a savage mumble,
and it lies just to keep in practice.
    There are things it will force you to see.

It promises to come back next week,
but you know it probably won't;
it is liable to get its throat cut
by another one just like it.
    It has settled on your life for good.

It shambles over the lawn
taking its own sweet time.
It can never be overworked;
it has a natural rhythm.
    It will stay. It will finally own you.

To Hear My Head Roar

First, my father taught me to read poetry
aloud; then my teachers in grade school
remembered how he had recited poetry,

how many times he had brought down the school-
house with "Casey at the Bat." Whenever they
could they called me up before the whole school

to be my father's son. I still dream of days they
stood me shaking before my classmates, then
waited while I launched into what they

knew from long experience was coming, then
sat through "Jabberwocky" or "Excelsior"—that was
the full range of my repertory then.

Later I almost liked it, though I was
still forced to it: each week we all recited
at assembly. A terrible, tiring time that was

for my audience, and for me, as I recited
"The Highwayman" and "The Cremation of
Sam McGee." My father coached as I recited

nightly in the living room, and on the day of
my graduation from that place, my sister
and I recited, respectively, "The Ballad of

the Harp-Weaver" and "The Highwayman." My sister
and I fled to our father's side after
it was over, and I can still see my sister

blushing as the old ladies came up after
the performance with tears in their eyes
to tell my father we were wonderful. After

that, it was a long time before my eyes
would follow the tricks of poems, but now I know
dozens of them: they unscroll behind my eyes,

and I own hundreds of books in which I know
I can always find the right thing at the right time,
and I will read to anyone who doesn't know

what he is in for, for hours at a time.
When I try to understand this part of myself,
I think back to that earlier, troublesome time

to find that the explanation of myself
does not lie there entirely; for now I recall being
in high school, just beginning to take myself

seriously, and my father as a human being,
and I think of hours I spent in the attic
rummaging through old file cases, being

surprised to find, in the dark dust of that attic,
the poems my father had written when he
was in college. One afternoon in the attic

yielded an ancient treasure, a recording he
had once made and then forgotten. I
tiptoed out of the attic with it, thinking he

might take it from me, and secretly I
tried it, at first without success, on the machine
downstairs in the living room. At last I

even tried to start the reluctant machine
on the inner end of the groove. It worked.
The thing had been cut on some amateur's machine

and was made to run from the inside out. I worked
with the needle, nudging it over the cracks,
and heard, after what seemed hours of work,

a voice that I recognized, through dusty cracks
and thirty years, as my father's (or my own), say
something I now take to heart as my heart cracks:

"This is Tom Taylor talking; talking," I heard him say,
"to hear his own voice, and reading some poetry
because he wants to have something to say."

RIDING A ONE-EYED HORSE

One side of his world is always missing.
You may give it a casual wave of the hand
or rub it with your shoulder as you pass,
but nothing on his blind side ever happens.

Hundreds of trees slip past him into darkness,
drifting into a hollow hemisphere
whose sounds you will have to try to explain.
Your legs will tell him not to be afraid

if you learn never to lie. Do not forget
to turn his head and let what comes come seen:
he will jump the fences he has to if you swing
toward them from the side that he can see

and hold his good eye straight. The heavy dark
will stay beside you always; let him learn
to lean against it. It will steady him
and see you safely through diminished fields.

LANDSCAPE WITH TRACTOR

How would it be if you took yourself off
to a house set well back from a dirt road,
with, say, three acres of grass bounded
by road, driveway, and vegetable garden?

Spring and summer you would mow the field,
not down to lawn, but with a bushhog,
every six weeks or so, just often enough
to give grass a chance, and keep weeds down.

And one day—call it August, hot, a storm
recently past, things green and growing a bit,
and you're mowing, with half your mind
on something you'd rather be doing, or did once.

Three rounds, and then on the straight
alongside the road, maybe three swaths in
from where you are now, you glimpse it. People
will toss all kinds of crap from their cars.

It's a clothing-store dummy, for God's sake.
Another two rounds, and you'll have to stop,
contend with it, at least pull it off to one side.
You keep going. Two rounds more, then down

off the tractor, and Christ! Not a dummy, a corpse.
The field tilts, whirls, then steadies as you run.
Telephone. Sirens. Two local doctors use pitchforks
to turn the body, some four days dead, and ripening.

And the cause of death no mystery: two bullet holes
in the breast of a well-dressed black woman
in perhaps her mid-thirties. They wrap her,
take her away. You take the rest of the day off.

Next day, you go back to the field, having
to mow over the damp dent in the tall grass
where bluebottle flies are still swirling,
but the bushhog disperses them, and all traces.

Weeks pass. You hear at the post office
that no one comes forward to say who she was.
Brought out from the city, they guess, and dumped
like a bag of beer cans. She was someone,

and now is no one, buried or burned
or dissected; but gone. And I ask you
again, how would it be? To go on with your life,
putting gas in the tractor, keeping down thistles,

and seeing, each time you pass that spot,
the form in the grass, the bright yellow skirt,
black shoes, the thing not quite like a face
whose gaze blasted past you at nothing

when the doctors heaved her over? To wonder,
from now on, what dope deal, betrayal,
or innocent refusal, brought her here,
and to know she will stay in that field till you die?

Taking to the Woods

Clearing brush away
is the mean part of working up firewood from these
cut-off treetops—a chaotic souvenir
of the doubtful covenant I made the day
I marked a dozen white oak trees
and sold them for veneer.

There might be more in this
of character or courage if it were need that drove
my weekly trials in this little wood,
but this is amateur thrift, a middle-class
labor as much for solitude
as for a well-stocked stove.

For more than safety's sake,
therefore, I take a break to light up and daydream,
and as the chainsaw ticks and cools, I smoke
my way back to an hour spent years ago,
when I knelt above a shallow stream—
the scanty overflow

from the springhouse at my back.
The ache of holding still dwindled away to less
than the absent-minded effort that has carved
these grooves between my eyebrows; on the surface
oarlocked water-striders swerved
above the scribbled black

shadows minnows made
on rippled mud below their bright formations,
and a dragonfly, the green-eyed snakedoctor
with wings out of old histories of aviation,
backed and filled down a stair of nectar-
scent toward a jewelweed

and struck a brittle stillness
like the spell the wood boss broke when he touched my hand
    as I stood absorbed in the loggers' technique:
    "Have you ever seen a big tree fall?" "Yes."
        "Good." Not the graceful faint we make
        of tall trees in the mind,

        but swift and shattering.
I counted the growth rings—one hundred sixty-four—
    and found where, fifty years ago, the wood
    drew in against the drought one narrow ring;
        I touched the band that marked the year
        when I was born, then stood

        and let them drop the rest.
This is everyday danger, mundane spectacle,
    spectacular and dangerous all the same.
    I hover between hope that it is practical
        to give young trees more light, and shame
        at laying old trees waste,

        then yank the starting cord
and turn to dropping stovewood from this chest-high limb,
    my touch light, leaving real work to the saw,
    my concentration thorough and ignored
        at once, lest the blade take on a whim
        of its own; and I think how

        our small towns have collected
in legend the curious deaths of ordinary men—
    as once, on a siding up the road from here,
    Jim Kaylor, if that was his name, directed
        the coupling of a single freight car
        to the middle of a train—

an intricacy he knew
as most of us know how to shave, say, or shift gears.
   That day, he managed to be caught somehow,
   and the couplings clicked inside him, just below
      the ribcage, and he hung between cars
         in odd silence as the crew

         swarmed from the depot,
told each other to stand back, give him air, send
   for the doctor, and he asked for a cigarette,
   received it with steady fingers, smoked, and saw—
      well, what could he have seen? The end
         of a boxcar, the set

         of a face in disbelief,
or something, in smoke shapes before him, that he kept
   when he finished the cigarette, flicked it aside,
   nodded, and, as the boxcars were slipped
      apart, dropped with a sound of relief
         to the crossties, and died.

      Now I think hard for men
mangled by tractors and bulls, or crushed under trees
   that fall to ax or chainsaw in their season,
   and for myself, who for no particular reason
      so far survive, to watch the woodlot ease
         under the dark again,

         withdraw into the mist
of my unfocused eyes, into my waiting stare
   across bare trees that lift toward landscapes
   through which snakedoctors may still wheel to rest,
      then to walk home, behind the shapes
         my breath ghosts in sharp air.

Airing Linen

Wash and dry,
sort and fold:
you and I
are growing old.

Barbed Wire

One summer afternoon when nothing much
was happening, they were standing around
a tractor beside the barn while a horse
in the field poked his head between two strands
of the barbed-wire fence to get at the grass
along the lane, when it happened—something

they passed around the wood stove late at night
for years, but never could explain—someone
may have dropped a wrench into the toolbox
or made a sudden move, or merely thought
what might happen if the horse got scared, and
then he did get scared, jumped sideways and ran

down the fence line, leaving chunks of his throat
skin and hair on every barb for ten feet
before he pulled free and ran a short way
into the field, stopped and planted his hoofs
wide apart like a sawhorse, hung his head
down as if to watch his blood running out,

almost as if he were about to speak
to them, who almost thought he could regret
that he no longer had the strength to stand,
then shuddered to his knees, fell on his side,
and gave up breathing while the dripping wire
hummed like a bowstring in the splintered air.

THE FLYING CHANGE

1

The canter has two stride patterns, one on the right
lead and one on the left, each a mirror image of the
other. The leading foreleg is the last to touch the
ground before the moment of suspension in the air.
On cantered curves, the horse tends to lead with the
inside leg. Turning at liberty, he can change leads
without effort during the moment of suspension, but
a rider's weight makes this more difficult. The aim of
teaching a horse to move beneath you is to remind
him how he moved when he was free.

2

A single leaf turns sideways in the wind
in time to save a remnant of the day;
I am lifted like a whipcrack to the moves
I studied on that barbered stretch of ground,
before I schooled myself to drift away

from skills I still possess, but must outlive.
Sometimes when I cup water in my hands
and watch it slip away and disappear,
I see that age will make my hands a sieve;
but for a moment the shifting world suspends

its flight and leans toward the sun once more,
as if to interrupt its mindless plunge
through works and days that will not come again.
I hold myself immobile in bright air,
sustained in time astride the flying change.

Hawk

Last year I learned to speak to a red-tail hawk.
He wheeled above me as I crossed a field;
he screamed; I pulled a blade of grass, set it
against my lips, and started screaming back.

We held that conversation for half a mile.
Once in a while he calls me out of the house
and I comb a border for the right blade of grass.
I used to wish I might learn what it is

we mean to one another; now, I keep
the noise we've mastered for itself alone,
for glimpses of his descent toward dead elms,
and a heart that will not mind when I am gone.

At the Swings

Midafternoon in Norfolk,
late July. I am taking our two sons for a walk
    away from their grandparents' house; we have
    directions to a miniature playground,
        and I have plans to wear them down
            toward a nap at five,

            when my wife and I
will leave them awhile with her father. A few blocks
    south of here, my wife's mother drifts from us
    beneath hospital sheets, her small strength bent
        to the poisons and the rays they use
            against a spreading cancer.

        In their house now, deep love
is studying to live with deepening impatience
    as each day gives our hopes a different form

and household tasks rise like a powdery mist
    or restless fatigue. Still, at five,
       my wife and I will dress

      and take the boulevard
across the river to a church where two dear friends
    will marry; rings will be blessed, promises kept
    and made, and while our sons lie down to sleep,
      the groom's niece, as the flower girl,
       will almost steal the show.

      But here the boys have made
an endless procession on the slides, shrieking down
    slick steel almost too hot to touch; and now
    they charge the swings. I push them from the front,
      one with each hand, until at last
       the rhythm, and the sunlight

      that splashes through live oak
and crape myrtle, dappling dead leaves on the ground,
    lull me away from this world toward a state
    still and remote as an old photograph
      in which I am standing somewhere
       I may have been before:

      there was this air, this light,
a day of thorough and forgetful happiness;
    where was it, or how long ago? I try
    to place it, but it has gone for good,
      to leave me gazing at these swings,
       thinking of something else

      I may have recognized—
an irrecoverable certainty that now,
    and now, this perfect afternoon, while friends
    are struggling to put on their cutaways
      or bridal gowns, and my wife's mother,
       dearer still, is dozing

after her medicine,
or turning a small thing in her mind, like someone
    worrying a ring of keys to make small sounds
    against great silence, and while these two boys
        swing back and forth against my hand,
            time's crosshairs quarter me

        no matter where I turn.
Now it is time to go. The boys are tired enough,
    and my wife and I must dress and go to church.
    Because I love our friends, and ceremony,
        the usual words will make me weep:
            hearing the human prayers

        for holy permanence
will remind me that a life is much to ask
    of anyone, yet not too much to give
    to love. And once or twice, as I stand there,
        that dappled moment at the swings
            will rise between the lines,

        when I beheld our sons
as, in the way of things, they will not be again,
    though even years from now their hair may lift
    a little in the breeze, as if they stood
        somewhere along their way from us,
            poised for a steep return.

A GRACE

once again, for Sarah

I give thanks for the way our kitchen dance
takes on the familiarity of ritual,
from the moment of decision, reached
in a mixture of eagerness and relief—
you'll roast a chicken, maybe, or

walk us both toward *boeuf carbonnade*—
through the several subtasks
we can or cannot help each other do,
and we quiet down, hearing small
sounds of lettuce being torn,
prunes snipped in quarters,
the nearly silent bristles
of the mushroom brush—
and then the table set and served,
the centering on a moment of hope
and gratitude, as once again
we face each other, having done
a small and daily kind of work
in a large, eternal kind of joy.

FLYING OVER PEORIA

for Louis Simpson

The man beside me nudges my arm
and shrugs toward the window.
"Peoria," he says. I glance across him
at clouds and vague patches of earth.
"Where many things won't play,"
I say, trying to smile.

His head sinks into the seat back.
"I lived there for three years,"
he says, "thirty years ago."
He stares ahead; I don't know what to say.
It's none of my business.
"Funny," he goes on,
"but I've forgotten it, in a way.
I mean it's hard for me to believe
I lived there. *I Lived in Peoria*—
like a concept, you know?
Oh, I remember things,

little scenes, like snapshots.
God, I even remember the milkman's name,
and I only saw him once.
I had a job there, friends, a life,
and I don't remember what it was like.
My job took me away."

He won't say any more. He is
about to cry. Does he want to,
or is he trying not to?

At this point in too many poems,
I, whoever that might be,
would think of embracing him,
but it rarely happens. A man weeps
privately, another ponders
odd uses of a word like *concept*,
and below them the featureless landscape
keeps slipping farther away.

UNDERSTANDING FICTION

What brings it to mind this time? The decal
from East Stroudsburg State in the window
ahead of me as traffic winds to the airport?

Maybe we pass the Stroudwater Landing apartments.
Whatever it is, you who are with me get to hear it
all over again: how once, just out of college

or maybe a year or two later, into the first
teaching job, some circumstance found me
in the home of an old friend, one of the mentors

to whom I owe what I am, on one of those days
when the airwaves are filled with football.
We remember it now as four games, and swear

to one another, and to others, that this
is what happened. In the second game,
as men unpiled from a crowded scramble,

a calm voice remarked that Mike Stroud
had been in on the tackle, and we told
ourselves that we had heard the same thing

in the first game. Odd. So we listened,
or claimed to be listening, and drank,
and took what we were pleased to call notice.

Never an isolating or identifying shot,
just these brief observations of crowds:
Mike Stroud was in all four games.

An astonishing trick, a terrific story—
some plot of the color commentators,
a tribute to a friend with a birthday,

or maybe just a joke on the world.
I tell it at least four times a year,
and each time it is longer ago.

Mike Stroud, if he ever played football,
does not do so now, but he might
even have played only one game

that late fall day in—oh, 1967, let's say.
We were drinking. God knows what we heard.
But I tell it again, and see how

to help you believe it, so I make
some adjustment of voice or detail,
and the story strides into the future.

A VOLTAGE SPIKE

In a motel at the wavering boundary between
countryside and a town whose name I don't bother to recall,
I stare through a generous window toward a clearing

of some half a dozen acres, bordered in pine
and a few varieties of bare deciduous trees,
the farther ones scraggling above a darker band

of background—trees even farther away, or a low hill.
Brown grass and broomsedge almost conceal the clay.
In the foreground a buried-cable pedestal rises

like a steel mullein stalk beside a walnut tree.
As I relax my gaze to a passive blur, the trees
darken and close in around a passing thought,

and the empty field becomes the backdrop
for a daydream not quite willed, as from the woods
come several dozen men in coveralls and stocking caps.

They carry clubs—of wood or metal, I can't be sure—
and move toward the center of the field.
With stolid care they set to killing one another:

the clubs rise and fall to a steady, thoughtful rhythm,
methodically cracking faces, bones, and skulls.
No one groans or shouts as the bodies drop;

even the sound of labored breathing is oddly faint.
I come to myself taking quick and shallow breaths,
my hands trying to crush the arms of the chair,

my eyes blinking to dissolve the savage tableau.
A light wind sways the broomsedge, and a flock
of starlings settles down like a cast of seeds.

After a Movie

The last small credits fade
as house lights rise. Dazed in that radiant instant
of transition, you dwindle through the lobby
and out to curbside, pulling on a glove
with the decisive competence
of the scarred detective

or his quarry. Scanning
the rainlit street for taxicabs, you visualize,
without looking, your image in the window
of the jeweler's shop, where white hands hover
above the string of luminous pearls
on a faceless velvet bust.

Someone across the street
enters a bar, leaving behind a charged vacancy
in which you cut to the dim booth inside,
where you are seated, glancing at the door.
You lift an eyebrow, recognizing
the unnamed colleague

who will conspire with you
against whatever the volatile script provides. . . .
A cab pulls up. You stoop into the dark
and settle toward a version of yourself.
Your profile cruises past the city
on a home-drifting stream

through whose surface, sometimes,
you glimpse the life between the streambed and the ripples,
as, when your gestures are your own again,
your fingers lift a cup beyond whose rim
a room bursts into clarity
and light falls on all things.

NIGHT SEARCH FOR LOST DOG

Not yet midnight, but late, and in through the window
the sound of a fox barking often and not far away
made me sit up and strain for something else, a clue
to the disappearance, two days before, of a silly old dog;

maybe they were out there in some kind of standoff.
High whining under the odd crystalline barking
made me think she was caught on the fence through the woods.
So up, into clothes, the hickory walking stick Larry Higgins

whittled for me, and I went out into the late winter night,
the sky high overcast and giving back from somewhere
more light than I would have believed possible this time
of night and year, easy walking down the hill to the woods,

and there it was again, out the driveway and off
to the left, where I went then, onto gravel and clay
packed almost to pavement, not hard to walk quietly,
and the drive stretched along through the trees

as it seems to have done once in an old illustration
in a book my grandparents had. It was something like that,
since the sight of it made me stop and go soft at the center
that a landscape so long gone could still be there

under my feet, winding out to the clearing
where the fox barked again, just there where the drive
comes out of the trees. Quicker then, still quiet,
I took one step at a time, stopping once at a sound,

a faint rhythmic thumping that turned out, probably,
to be a wrinkle in the nylon parka working against
my own pulse beating somewhere inside it, so I went on
to the big field on the right, past the woods,

to the place in the fence where the barbed wire
will hold a climber with a stout stick to prop him,

and the fox galloped freely away over the hill.
After a while it was just myself standing there,

hearing for the first time the racket from the house
on the opposite hill, young hounds maybe sensing
someone walking and climbing as quietly as his age
and a noisy down parka would allow, but not knowing,

maybe, that he was looking for a dog who was born here
and stayed for eleven years, learning little, but loved,
then one day was simply not there. No sign of a fight
or the hoped-for standoff with the fox, or a coon,

rabid or not, the thought of which had prompted the stick
now supporting two folded hands, my chin resting on them,
my eyes going in and out of focus on a world that right then
it was good, after all, to be in, mystified though I was, and sad.

AFTERNOONS WITH A BOOMERANG

        An insect afternoon
of annoyance, discontent, the vain wish to be
    far away, and I sit on the patio
      staring at lawn, woods, receding green patches
        with the impossible loveliness
          of vanished children's books—

        yet here it is around me,
consoling if not healing; I know no kinder place
    in which to bear involuntary gloom.
      Then across the patio comes a blur,
        red shorts, legs, arms, three strides to grass
          and I can focus now

        on Richard, coming out
from under the weight of his own troubles, his hand

cocked, gripping a bright handmade boomerang
that now he throws, like a knife at a target.
    For sixty instantaneous feet
        it flies straight, then yanks left

    and banks upward, tilting
into level flight, a spun, evanescent circle
    back to the house, then toward another sweep
    by the woods, flickering in and out of view
        against backgrounds of sycamore
            and maple, sky and grass—

    a flutter of silence
to where he pirouettes, watching the cycle close
    as the end of the spiral drops within reach
    and he plucks it from air. Our separate woes
        may not pass for more than a moment,
            but this is the moment.

    Not that he never misses:
the stick will spin too hard to be caught, or a stray
    current of air from the woods grabs an edge,
    or he has to look into the sun. Sometimes
        the gravel driveway breaks his stride
            over the dampening grass.

    Twenty minutes, half an hour,
and his arm tires; still, it always feels like forever,
    infinite small variations within
    the aboriginal pattern, and I think
        that whatever their use among hunters,
            artists most deeply own

        these physical mysteries
of getting a skill right, or nearly so, or, rarely,
    of getting it wrong, the shout going up
    at the botched release, the sharp smile of disgust
        as the boomerang goes off course
            and snags itself in a tree.

Error and correction,
flight and return, my son pulling hard as he can
    toward making a life that is his, lifting
    himself a little from his private griefs,
        and me, for a while, out of mine—
            and though the pain returns,

        he gives, in fading light,
a look of birthright ease to a difficult thing.
    Whatever unrolls on this spiral path,
    lifelong though it may be, and hard, is worth no more,
        in the end, than these crystal instants
            of grace and lighthearted awe.

Acknowledgments

The poems by FRED CHAPPELL included herein appeared in the following volumes: *The World Between the Eyes* (Louisiana State University Press, 1971), copyright © 1963, 1964, 1966, 1969, 1970, 1971 by Fred Chappell; *River* (Louisiana State University Press, 1975), copyright © 1975 by Fred Chappell; *Wind Mountain* (Louisiana State University Press, 1979), copyright © 1979 by Fred Chappell; *Source* (Louisiana State University Press, 1985), copyright © 1985 by Fred Chappell; *First and Last Words* (Louisiana State University Press, 1989), copyright © 1989 by Fred Chappell; *C* (Louisiana State University Press, 1993), copyright © 1978, 1980, 1982, 1983, 1986, 1988, 1989, 1990, 1992, 1993 by Fred Chappell; and *Spring Garden: New and Selected Poems* (Louisiana State University Press, 1995), copyright © 1995 by Fred Chappell.

The poems by KELLY CHERRY included herein appeared in the following volumes: *Lovers and Agnostics* (1975; rpr. Carnegie-Mellon University Press, 1995), copyright © 1975, 1995 by Kelly Cherry; *Relativity: A Point of View* (Louisiana State University Press, 1977), copyright © 1977 by Kelly Cherry; *Natural Theology* (Louisiana State University Press, 1988), copyright © 1973, 1975, 1976, 1977, 1978, 1979, 1980, 1981, 1982, 1983, 1988 by Kelly Cherry; *God's Loud Hand* (Louisiana State University Press, 1993), copyright © 1974, 1975, 1976, 1977, 1979, 1980, 1983, 1985, 1987, 1988, 1989, 1990, 1991, 1992, 1993 by Kelly Cherry; and *Time Out of Mind* (chapbook; March Street Press, 1994), copyright © 1994 by Kelly Cherry. *Lovers and Agnostics* was originally published in 1975 by Red Clay Books.

The poems by R. H. W. DILLARD included herein appeared in the following volumes: *The Day I Stopped Dreaming about Barbara Steele and Other Poems* (The University of North Carolina Press, 1966), copyright © 1965, 1966 by R. H. W. Dillard; *News of the Nile* (The University of North Carolina Press, 1971), copyright © 1967, 1968, 1969, 1971 by R. H. W. Dillard; *After Borges* (Louisiana State University Press, 1972), copyright © 1972 by R. H. W. Dillard; *The First Man on the Sun* (Louisiana State University Press, 1983), copyright © 1983 by R. H. W. Dillard; *Greeting* (University of Utah Press, 1981), copyright © 1965, 1966, 1967, 1968,